HR
Effectiveness

Jim Matthewman is Consultancy Director of HR-BC, a group specialising in the introduction of quality HR practice and procedures. He has advised over 2,000 organisations, both public and private, on topics like absence policy, computerisation, payment systems and equal value. He lectures regularly to universities, MBA courses, the IPD, CBI and Institute of Directors. He was editor of *Industrial Relations in Practice* and *Human Resource: Management and Strategy* and author of books such as the *IDS Guide to Job Evaluation* and *Controlling Absenteeism*.

HR
Effectiveness

Jim Matthewman

INSTITUTE OF PERSONNEL AND DEVELOPMENT

Typesetting by Photoprint, Torquay
and printed in Great Britain by
Short Run Press, Exeter

British Library Cataloguing in Publication Data

Matthewman, Jim
 HR Effectiveness. – (Developing
Strategies Series)
 I. Title II. Series
 658.3

 ISBN 0–85292–570–0

The views expressed in this book are the author's own, and
may not necessarily reflect those of the IPM.

iÞ

**INSTITUTE OF PERSONNEL
AND DEVELOPMENT**

IPD House, Camp Road, London SW19 4UX
Tel: 081 946 9100   Fax: 081 947 2570
Registered office as above. Registered Charity No. 1038333
A company limited by guarantee. Registered in England No. 2931892

▞ Contents

CASE STUDIES

Acknowledgements

I am very grateful to colleagues past and present who have encouraged me to put pen to paper and I hope that this text will give personnel practitioners a means of reviewing their own function and ways of improving the service they provide to their organisations as a whole. This book has been based on my experiences advising over 2,000 organisations in the UK and Europe, and reflects my view that, in most cases, there is considerable scope to improve the effectiveness of personnel and human resource activity.

I would like to give thanks to a number of people who have supported and backed my ideas over the years, notably: the team at HR-BC especially Clare Hogg and Iris Bedford; Dave Martin, Beth Dugan, John Angel, Alan Flett; and most of all my family, Suzi, Miles and Gemma.

In addition I must extend special thanks to the following who have made major contributions to this book:

- Graham Medcroft — Human Resources Director, Edmund Nuttall Ltd.
- Andrew Mayo — Director of Human Resource Development, ICL Europe
- John Cooper — Director of Training & Development, Bull UK
- John Beadle — Compensation & Benefits Manager, Glaxo
- David McCammon — Personnel Executive, KLM Royal Dutch Airlines.

Finally, I must acknowledge the vast number of personnel practitioners I have met over the years who have been prepared to share their different views, problems and goals with me. It is this variety which makes personnel such a fascinating discipline.

List of Figures

▨ Introduction

We all like our efforts to be recognised and respected by others. Yet sometimes work within the personnel and human resource function can seem pretty frustrating. Too often personnel people feel under pressure, under-resourced and, many I guess, underpaid for the efforts put in. These feelings can be even more acute if the department is openly criticised or lacks respect. Decisions made elsewhere are given to Personnel to implement. Many may be unpopular and the function bears the brunt.

Respect comes from credibility. Credibility in turn is a reflection of effectiveness, presentation and influence. This is what this book is about.

In many cases how Personnel is viewed is simply a result of the way the department has been organised and the way we do things, but sometimes it is down to the way we communicate and present ideas or initiatives to our clients. I am totally convinced of the importance of personnel/human resources to the achievement of business goals – and this means getting close to your clients and understanding them.

This book examines why it is important to raise the personnel department's profile and how the function can quantify its value to the organisation. Effectiveness is about meeting goals and targets. These need to be agreed and tangible evidence provided to show progress towards the targets. However, for many personnel departments such targets have been less than clear and most lack any means of measurement. This book looks at how your department can review performance.

Reviewing Personnel performance raises another question: who judges effectiveness? Overall it must be the organisation and those who manage it. But there are many clients of Personnel: the board and senior executives, line managers, individual employees, and external applicants. So part of the answer must involve being able to identify who these clients are and what they expect from the department. This can be difficult as different groups have, not surprisingly, differing needs and priorities.

Traditionally, Personnel has sought to deliver a service to all employees, adopting an 'all-comers welcomed' philosophy. But organisations' needs have changed rapidly over the past decade, and the fact that many personnel functions have changed their name to 'human resources' reflects a need for the function clearly to align its goals with those of the business. The reality is that, while human resources is often seen as a prime agent of organisational change, the department itself needs to undergo major cultural change. Again, I hope this book will provide some insight into how to incorporate change *within* the function.

How to use this book

The book is aimed at all personnel departments – especially those in small- to medium-sized organisations (i.e. those employing between 250 and 1,000 employees). Even so, my experience has shown that personnel departments in some of the UK's largest organisations would benefit equally from adopting a regular HR audit, a programme of improvement and a desire to raise the quality of service delivered. Many of our famous blue-chip names have no reason to feel complacent in the current climate. Every improvement is worthwhile and will add to the effectiveness of the department.

At each stage I have tried to identify the areas which need to be examined, ways of measuring performance and how to act on the results. I hope this will provide a practical framework for your organisation. If you feel that the task is just too great and potentially too costly to your business, I would ask you to consider the alternative cost and impact of not pursuing a goal of improved efficiency and effectiveness. But it does demand commitment.

If you feel that you need to gain some practice and

confidence first, my advice is to choose one or two specific areas of personnel activity and use these to pilot an audit and improvement programme. In this way every personnel department can make progress.

I have included five case studies (Chapters 5–9), where the HR/personnel departments have gained high internal respect for the way they have implemented change to their function. I believe each exemplifies a sound basis of how to get things right. I would have liked to included many more had space and time allowed.

1

▓ Pressure on the HR Function

Many personnel/human resource functions are showing signs of insecurity, desperately searching for an identity and justification within their organisation. As a service function, HR/Personnel is well aware that it plays primarily a supporting role to the main business and therefore needs to be seen to deliver something that contributes to overall value.

In the present climate many organisations are under severe pressure due to reduced revenue, and their current existence is largely dependent on tight control of overheads. For the majority this has meant cutbacks in terms of budgets, resources, equipment or premises.

The personnel function often has a poor image – sometimes justified but in the main due to its lack of internal marketing and presentation. Now under the spotlight, the HR/personnel profession is anxiously seeking ways to measure its effectiveness and demonstrate its contribution to bottom-line profitability. Ironically, some of its initiatives are undermining its perceived role. The current enthusiasm for performance management and empowerment, which seeks to delegate and transfer more authority to operational line managers, also takes away many of the traditional management controls established by the personnel function.

To remain competitive, today's organisations, whether in the private or public sector, need to be flexible, lean and skilful. This has meant that traditional hierarchical management structures, with set reporting lines and closely defined job descriptions, are being replaced by business and project teams where individual roles are tailored to customer requirements. In these circumstances formal, rigid organisational and reward structures hinder operations. Control is measured by results.

In such a climate organisations are undergoing massive cultural change, and the personnel function not only needs to take part in the change but should be a prime agent of it. This

1

means that Personnel's role needs to develop significantly in order to meet these challenges.

Increasing pressures

There have been three rising pressures on personnel practitioners:

- Self-preservation
- The need to be seen to be effective
- The drive for quality management, either as part of a Total Quality Management (TQM) initiative or for ISO 9000/BS 5750 certification.

First, the length and depth of the present recession has forced most companies to rationalise operations resulting in an attendant need to reduce numbers of staff. With moves to teamwork and shared knowledge, many organisations have sought to de-layer management structures and reduce dependence on specialists. The personnel department is no exception. Many corporate headquarters have radically cut the number of HR specialists and have returned these responsibilities to local personnel staff or operational line managers. The size of the corporate umbrella is now under question and as a result some senior personnel positions are under threat.

In the eyes of many operational managers, the personnel function does not provide a credible service. Too often the department is accused of being:

- Insular
- Bureaucratic
- Reactive
- Rigid and process-driven

and not:

- Business-oriented
- Responsive
- Proactive and strategic
- Flexible.

Furthermore, the personnel profession is portrayed as slow, cumbersome, and cautious even though, in reality, many are championing exciting, innovative people initiatives. This appears to stem from two sources. First, the roots of Human Resources are in welfare and personnel administration, and it still remains a clerically intensive occupation, thriving on policies, procedures and forms. Second, training has often been an off-shoot, if not a separate section. Many of the innovative and novel HR initiatives have been associated with people development. Here the national reform of training programmes and vocational qualifications has encouraged new ideas, notably competency-based strategies, plus a heightened awareness of skill as a major resource for competitive advantage. The apparent divorce between Personnel and training/development, both within companies and at a professional level, has in some respects exposed the lack of change within day-to-day personnel management.

The pace of change is also evident in the way the personnel function has responded to new technology. Operational staff will usually be the first to benefit from new hardware or software systems. Personnel remains the Cinderella function when seeking new systems within the department. This is because of:

- poorly defined requirements
- inability to present strong business justification
- lack of budget approval
- failure to identify and deliver benefits to clients.

Partly through frustration and partly through a desire to

maintain confidentiality, personnel systems tend to be solely for departmental use. This means that Personnel has had to justify a budget on its own merit, usually where no provision has been made. Recent research suggests (see *Personnel Management*, June 1993) that only 73 per cent of all organisations had use of computerised personnel systems. Of all those who did, two-thirds were using the systems as electronic filing cabinets and only one-third claimed 'strategic use'; the majority were failing to make use of their system's potential.

A change is about to occur. More organisations are now looking for integrated solutions (usually personnel and payroll) and some are actively seeking systems which can provide line manager access.

All too often Personnel has failed to live up to its promise to deliver 'high-quality management information'. In some cases line managers have even started to develop their own database systems in order to obtain personnel information. So while there is much talk and a considerable number of articles claiming moves to 'proactive' personnel management, there remains little tangible evidence. Indeed, it is hard to see how this could be otherwise when many personnel professionals find it difficult to identify their internal clients and what each expects of the function.

In this setting, therefore, Personnel must look to improve both its service level and its profile to ensure value to the organisation – and associated recognition. Within the public sector, personnel functions are now coming to terms with Service Level Agreements whereby the department must set the service standards it will provide to its user departments. This is in the face of direct competition from commercial personnel consultancies who may now tender for certain services.

Third, a major influence has been the drive for quality within management processes. A significant proportion of organisations have introduced TQM programmes, which by definition must include personnel activities. As the recent IPM Report showed, personnel departments are often asked to lead or champion such schemes through their responsibility for communication strategy. Sensibly, any department charged with such a brief would do well to ensure that its own department is a showcase of best practice.

However, a larger number of organisations are involved in seeking ISO 9000/BS 5750 certification. This international quality standard measures the management processes involved in the design, production and delivery of products and services. The standard says very little in respect of obvious personnel activities other than a need to record and monitor training records. Recruitment and selection, employee relations, communication and remuneration are not specifically covered. (The standard is to be revised in 1996 and it is likely that more personnel activities will be incorporated.) As a result there are a number of companies which have BS 5750 recognition even though Personnel has not been actively involved.

On the other hand, a growing number of personnel departments within organisations seeking certification have decided to take on board the principles in order to improve their own procedures and to stay in line with other management functions. Furthermore the kudos, pride and satisfaction gained by other functions succeeding in quality improvement programmes has drawn envious desire from aspiring personnel managers and directors keen to achieve similar professional and business recognition.

Personnel must be seen to be effective

As the financial spotlight scans the organisation for potential cost savings, personnel departments often claim that they, like others, are being asked to do more for less. To maintain or justify resource levels, the department must be seen to be effective.

Line managers and senior executives have become more demanding. Increased delegation plus the introduction and utilisation of new technology has raised both the expectations and the speed of response required. Unfortunately, many existing personnel procedures are excessively bureaucratic. Paper is often demanded in triplicate, all with appropriate sign-off levels backed by financial and operational justifications. Duplication is also rife. Information is often transferred from one form to another, summarised on a record card and entered into a computer system. Information generated from computers is sometimes re-typed into another format. Information provided is often not in the client's desired format, rarely summarised and frequently includes too much to be easily assimilated. At this stage some may feel defensive, but this is not an overstatement for the majority of small to medium-sized organisations in the UK – and also applies to a significant number of blue-chip organisations I have dealt with.

In many cases the solution is quite simple, but busy personnel people rarely make or take the time to resolve the problem. It is likely that one or more of the situations above is currently happening in your personnel department. Yet there would be immediate improvements if only a graph could be generated or the personnel system could pass data directly to payroll. In my experience most departments have the equipment or systems to perform these tasks but, more often than not, the individuals responsible lack the skill, training or *direction* to achieve such immediate benefits.

My first recommendation, therefore, is that you ensure that your staff are trained and sufficiently skilled to take advantage of the technology available. A day's training on graphics or interface software will give immediate returns in terms of report quality and timesaving.

Over a period of eight years I oversaw the implementation of personnel software into over 1,500 organisations. All but a small handful spent most time inputting data (over 1,600 separate items per individual for one major organisation, yet the department only reported on 264 fields). Furthermore, the majority of companies did not store reports in the available reports library; most used the report generator to create *ad hoc* reports. This has two implications: first, clients expect instant answers to any request and this expectation is difficult to control, hence there will be times when the department struggles to meet the request; second, the immediacy of information might be sacrificed for quality in terms of checking the accuracy of data and its presentation. Credibility is quickly undermined if reports are of questionable accuracy or difficult to read.

To overcome these difficulties, the function should take the time to find out the key reports required from its main clients, check the frequency and format desired and then produce a quality management report pack on a monthly basis. This has the advantage of satisfying core information needs to desired quality levels and reducing the number of *ad hoc* reports to the department. This in turn will ensure that personnel staff have more time to plan, implement and monitor activity rather than forever chasing often repetitive requests.

So, my second recommendation is to ensure that the personnel function promotes a quality profile by identifying client report requirements, their frequency and ideal format in order to control both expectation and quality of presentation.

Finally, credibility is also a function of influence. Personnel needs to be seen to participate in the decision-making process at all levels. How is this demonstrated in management? A person is able to influence others by:

- Understanding and informed comment
- Power of argument (this may be by force or strength of commitment or by weight of argument, i.e. factual evidence and logical deduction)
- Winning allies prepared to sponsor or support a given strategy, usually because they too will benefit
- Chairperson's recommendation.

Unfortunately, Personnel's lack of representation on boards of directors (only 16 per cent of personnel directors or heads of department sit on executive boards) prevents direct access to

the key decision-making forum. This is not because Personnel
is less important (most boards are keen to emphasise the value
of employees as their key asset in corporate reports) but it may
reflect Personnel's poor marketing of HR activity.

Few personnel managers or directors in medium-sized companies seem to know or are able to state the corporate's short-
or medium-term objectives. It is fundamental that personnel
gets closer and aligns its policies to the core business goals –
this demands more understanding of business practice and,
ultimately, of profit and loss accounting.

Personnel often displays an alarming naivety in respect of
preparing proposals with an adequate business case. Major
initiatives or expenditures need clear cost/benefit arguments
that can illustrate a contribution to the business. They need to
take account of purchasing policy and approval mechanisms.
Few consultants and suppliers believe a personnel practitioner
who states that he or she has a budget allocated for a given
project. More usually a figure has been incorporated within a
departmental budget plan but approval will still require justification and a sign-off from the chief executive, board or finance
department.

In terms of weight of argument, Personnel needs to ensure
that tangible evidence is provided to support any proposal.
Personnel professionals need to present figures to show what is
actually required by the business, how the department pro-
poses to meet these needs, how the programme is to be
implemented, and how results will be monitored to ensure the
investment requested will give a valued return. Proof of
delivery will, in turn, improve credibility and so help to justify
further personnel/HR initiatives.

Winning allies demands open, receptive exchange of ideas,
flexibility and compromise so both parties gain. Personnel
departments need to apply their undoubted practice and skill
in negotiation of collective agreements and in dealing with
their management colleagues. Most of all, they need to get
CEO or MD sponsorship plus operational management sup-

port. Personnel needs to get out and about among these groups: to be visible and listening.

Ultimately, all personnel departments need to present strategies, proposals and initiatives attractively. This means presenting to an equivalent standard as, say, the marketing or sales function; it means presenting in appropriate management language (i.e. hard financial summaries, trends and variances) and in a fashion which can be assimilated quickly (i.e. graphically, supported by tables and commentary).

So a third recommendation is: review how the department presents major proposals; and ensure all programmes have clear cost/benefit arguments which are supported by line manager endorsements, full business analysis and factual evidence.

To succeed, the culture of the department must change. It needs to become client-oriented, outward-looking, responsive and, most of all, focused on results. Such change requires courage. The department needs to find out exactly what the organisation and its managers expect from personnel; it needs commitment to seek to improve areas of concern or criticism; it needs to set standards it can deliver; and to ensure that it meets those agreed service levels. All of this demands measurement, an area which is examined in detail in Chapter 2.

2

Why Measure HR Activities?

Effectiveness and measurement go hand in hand. The attempt to judge how effective the personnel function is assumes that there is a benchmark or some scale to refer to. Effectiveness is also used to describe performance but this not only demands clear goals and targets, it also requires monitoring.

Furthermore, effective implies well-managed. The Personnel Standards Lead Body in its report *A Perspective on Personnel* opens the chapter 'The Success of the Personnel Function' with the following words:

> Credibility is critical for the success of personnel: people at all levels will judge the function by the performance of those who staff it and by the way that it is managed.

The function needs to demonstrate why and how all resources are used but most personnel departments have rarely monitored how they use people, time or money. Unlike finance, there are no accepted conventions. Some feel uncomfortable with the notion that *all* activity can be measured and the quality of service assessed. This may be due to fear of the results or concern about how to go about it in the first place. For a great many I suspect that the latter applies.

There are also practitioners who believe personnel activity involves a lot of work where results are intangible and difficult to measure. While these results may not be so obvious, in truth any activity can be measured – and needs to be if standards are to be set and maintained. The difference is that the measure is likely to be based on clients' opinion or satisfaction. Asking others to judge the function's performance is, however, less comfortable, demands openness and invites criticism. In the past many personnel departments have remained insular and largely secretive.

The 1980s saw the rise of customer service as the key to business survival. Organisations recognise that, in increasingly competitive markets, responsible customer care not only ensures existing clients remain loyal but also acts as reference for new business. This is equally applicable to the personnel function in its dealings with its customers. The exposure to such programmes in many walks of life (witness the rise of 'charterism') has made the British people more critical where traditionally criticism was considered bad form. Secondly, line managers themselves have been subjected to exacting performance and quality assessment, and they, too, now feel justified in demanding and commenting on the quality of service provided by Personnel.

For these reasons internal clients quite rightly feel they can judge the effectiveness of the function in terms of standard and satisfaction levels. But this assumes that the function has both identified its internal clients, and publicised and agreed these standards.

The challenge of continuous improvement

The turbulence of economic life has had an impact on all organisations. For many people their employer seems to be in a constant state of reorganisation, lacking direction and displaying managerial inconsistency. For long-serving employees the lack of security and need for change has been traumatic. The personnel function has borne much of the brunt of these changes. It has had to implement organisational change, counsel employees and, where necessary, declare redundancies. For many people, including personnel staff, this has meant a move back to the traditional 'welfare function', with personnel having to balance its role in implementation with employee care.

Faced by these challenges, it is tempting to present change as a temporary adjustment necessary in the light of business pressures. The reality is somewhat different. Leading organisations now recognise that their success and survival depends on the ability to be flexible and adaptable. It also requires continuous improvement in results, productivity, cost control and quality.

This means that the personnel department needs to identify both what it is doing today and what it needs to take on for the future. To do so requires an audit of current activity plus identification of future needs/expectations *of the business*. Personnel must accept that the future is likely to be one of constant change. Policies and procedures will need to be more flexible and under continual revision. The function must also anticipate and manage change. This is easier to do if personnel practice and procedure has clarity and has been simplified (see Chapter 4).

Continuous improvement requires monitoring. This can only start once initial standards or benchmarks have been established. Monitoring also requires regular review and reporting. It is said that the most effective way of learning is taking account of your mistakes; unfortunately many management systems allow individuals to deflect blame so that difficulties or issues become the responsibility of others or of external events. Our society encourages such behaviour, although increased monitoring and performance management are actively seeking closer accountability.

The quality personnel department needs to strive for excellence, indeed for perfection. Each improvement towards this goal is worthwhile in helping to create a showcase of best practice. Continuous monitoring demands criticism and continual questioning of whether the current methods or policies are the most efficient or appropriate to meet future goals. This is easier to assess if benchmarks are established, thereby highlighting variance and trends.

To be credible, Personnel must have business and organisational imagination – this requires an ability to consider a wide perspective of strategy and policy, plus analytical skills to help others understand and interpret the impact on employees. If people and their roles are the key differentiators between one organisation and another in today's competitive climate, then Personnel should be the lead player in monitoring and advising how the business implements its strategies.

But success in strategy usually comes down to implementation. Some of the best plans and initiatives fall by the wayside simply through poor or inadequate implementation. Once again monitoring is the key – if the process of monitoring is not set up from the start, the programme may well be too far down the track before the warning signals can flag the issues and corrective action can be taken.

Too often Personnel has been guilty of championing radical change lacking a clear implementation or monitoring plan. Consequently, such evangelical enthusiasm can fall flat when good intentions are not equalled by results. It is critical that any major initiative starts with clear objectives, sets measurable targets, and closely monitors the introduction of and progress towards the goals. It is therefore fundamental that the personnel department ensures that all major initiatives are supported by an implementation plan which includes a specific monitoring programme.

I have already commented on the impact of change. Where many companies and personnel functions seem to falter is in seeing change as a temporary state. In over 17 years of dealing with UK organisations, I have only come across one organisation (ICL, see Chapter 5) where there is an acceptance of *continual change*. Furthermore, change is seen by ICL as the main opportunity for business growth and is, therefore, considered a positive influence rather than a negative, disruptive force.

The benefits of an HR audit for the personnel department

As Giles Holman stated in the *Personnel Management Essay 1985*, the real knack lies in predicting and being fully prepared for change. This means 'keeping ahead'; Holman defines this as making time to read, think and plan. But it also means identifying potential consequences before they occur. Through HR measurement, Personnel can spot trends and variances; it can then make informed judgements with a degree of confidence, and hence achieve credibility. This is the key benefit of a regular audit of the HR function.

The additional benefits of an HR audit can be summarised as follows:

- *Ability to prioritise activity.* Identifying what the department does, and what the business requires, will help Personnel assess how it balances potentially conflicting demands for its resources and effectively prioritises these requests. In the past many departments have tried to meet every request, regardless of priorities, and have been guilty of poor or lower service to all. Now with limited resources, time and money, everybody in the department needs to be highly focused. Too often HR audits are seen as cost-containing exercises – they are really opportunities for resource maximisation.
- *Exposing duplication of effort.* Traditionally Personnel has been clerically intensive. It has a natural affinity with procedures, forms and policies. It loves to maintain fall-back systems, so normally there is a full paper record of any data held electronically. Forms are often completed in duplicate, if not triplicate. Worse still, it often demands updates of information it already holds – all of which seriously undermines its credibility with line managers and employees alike. Without an audit how can Personnel be sure it has removed unnecessary duplication, re-working and inconsistency?
- *Clarity of purpose.* Many people working in larger HR departments have little knowledge of the overall personnel goals or indeed what others do. An audit helps identify what people *actually do*; it helps provide each person with a clarity of purpose and will reinforce teamwork and mutual

dependence. In turn, this is likely to provide increased professionalism, enhanced reputation and a marked improvement in job satisfaction – if only because someone has taken the trouble to find out and clarify what people do, why they do it, how well it's done, and recognise the frustrations and obstacles placed in front of staff.

- *Business focus.* Any HR audit needs to take as broad a perspective of the function as possible. This means not only reviewing the efficiency within the department but also assessing how personnel practice and policy affects the organisation as a whole. It needs to consider how the business rates current HR activity, areas of concern and hence potential improvement and, significantly, what the organisation expects of the function. By such appraisal, the function will inevitably become more closely aligned with the business philosophy and the organisation's goals, which in turn will ensure a move from an administrative function to a service geared to operational profitability.

The organisational payback

For the organisation, the returns from an audit are significant. The more closely aligned personnel practice is with operational needs, the more effective the organisation will be in adapting to customer and economic need. In practical terms this will be reflected in:

- *Better recruitment and selection.* More effective recruitment and selection will not only give better value for money, it is also likely to provide a better fit and hence more adaptable teams.
- *Better information.* Better information backed up by simple, clear procedures will reduce the amount of time line managers and supervisors (team leaders) need to spend on administering staff relations and hence provide more

time to be spent on qualitative staff development. Furthermore, as the information base improves, with more accurate and quicker retrieval, so responsiveness to *ad hoc* requests will also rise – thereby raising the quality of service provided.

- *Effective funding.* Improved appraisal and skill auditing will help line managers and the organisation assess the current skill base against future needs. Efficient administration and analysis will then help ensure that training investment is allocated to the areas of highest return to the company.

- *Resource utilisation.* For most organisations staff costs are the highest variable overhead, requiring responsible control. Too often companies focus solely on numbers (actual heads or equivalent FTEs). The real debate should centre around resource *maximisation*. It is Personnel's role to ensure that the organisation takes full advantage of the skills and effort available in its workforce. This means ensuring attendance and shift rostering is efficient and cost-effective. Secondly, Personnel must also make certain that line managers are fully aware of employees' existing and potential skills. To fulfil either role, accurate data is essential.

The international dimension

I have said that Personnel needs to take the widest perspective in anticipating change. For many this necessitates a move from a traditional departmental focus to business and customer-orientation. But it should also adopt an international outlook for two further reasons.

First, Britain's membership of the European Community (EC) demands that Personnel keeps abreast of any employment legislation and initiatives being implemented, or under consideration, within all Member States. Britain's history of voluntary guidance and best practice (exemplified through numerous ACAS and IPD codes) is increasingly under threat from European legislative requirements. A credible personnel function must be seen to be informed and advisory, thereby helping organisations anticipate the likely impact of proposed EC measures.

Second, the increasing globalisation of markets, enhanced through technology and competition, again demands that the personnel function reacts quickly to international opportunities (e.g. new markets in Eastern Europe or South-East Asia) or to potential acquisition, merger or joint venture with international partners.

Both of these aspects of the international dimension demand flexibility and adaptability. Policies and practice need to be malleable so that strategic decisions are not hindered by a procedural bureaucracy unable to keep pace. This flexibility is more likely if personnel procedures are specifically designed to be both simple and subject to review. An audit should be able to test how flexible these are in practice: in essence how responsive and sensitive the function is in given circumstances. A forward-thinking function should try to anticipate and keep the following areas under review:

- *Technological change.* The department needs to be fully aware of developing IT strategies both in computerisation and communications. It needs to understand how it might be able to take advantage of these new advances (especially in respect of communications, e.g. use of E-Mail).
- *Potential cultural change.* It needs to understand the likely implications of mergers, foreign parent companies and joint ventures. This is best achieved by contacting and visiting organisations operating in such environments and considering how this might impact on your own company.
- *Identification of constraint.* The audit will also highlight which areas of personnel activity are potentially responsive to change and those which would be harder to alter, and why.

The culture of Personnel

In many cases Personnel finds that, because of the way the function is perceived, initiating change can be very frustrating. Traditionally Personnel has been a welfare and administrative unit. Line managers and employees (some with very long memories) may still demand and expect a caring, counselling service, especially in terms of reorganisation and restructuring, and this can hamper the function's ability to present itself as a prime agent of change.

Equally the function needs to manage expectations carefully. All too often personnel initiatives become widely enthusiastic missions implemented without full line commitment and with unrealistic expectations that fail to materialise both in time and results.

To resolve these problems, the personnel function needs to agree its goals and objectives with operational management. It needs to ensure that its own staff understand the goals and objectives and that they are widely publicised. It is alarming how many people, both within the department and its clients, are unable to define the role or purpose of the function.

In many organisations the personnel department is viewed as:

- Traditional in outlook
- Bureaucratic
- Process-driven
- Slow to respond
- Lightweight
- Controlling
- Operational rather than strategic.

Often these opinions are held strongly, irrespective of whether they are accurate or not. In part this is due to the fact that most employees and line managers can recall an individual incident or crisis, usually personal (for example, disciplinary hearings, redundancy or pay announcements, grading or grievance appeals) in which, more often than not, Personnel is seen in a negative light.

The personnel department, therefore, should include some form of attitude/satisfaction survey of its clients and compare the results against its own perceptions. Not only will these comparisons be extremely informative in their own right but they may also help explain why some of the best employee initiatives fail to deliver their expected rewards.

Identifying the internal clients

Most believe that Personnel is a service department. As such it needs to have a clear idea of:

- Who the department's clients are
- What they need and expect from Personnel
- Some measure to gauge how well the department is meeting their demands.

Many managers and employees openly express frustration and exasperation with Personnel's apparently endless collation of data but frequent inability to provide information on request. In some cases departmental managers have now started to set up their own systems, forms and reports – further undermining Personnel's credibility.

Not all internal clients are equal. Unfortunately many personnel practitioners, especially those involved in personnel administration, act as if they are. The dangers can be that trying to meet all-comers through an open-door policy results in little available time to plan, implement and present more proactive or strategic aims. This can result in an image of constant fire-fighting and an appearance of ineffectual chaos.

The solution to this problem lies in the prioritisation of activity based on a ranking of internal clients. To make an impact and to win credibility, the function needs to understand what each client group requires, to assess the most appropriate means of delivery and presentation, and to allocate resources accordingly. For many personnel departments, priorities are often dictated by expediency (i.e. time deadlines) without sufficient and equal weight being placed on the quality of service provided.

Most departmental reports are listings or word-processed documents. The majority are lengthy, difficult to digest and factual rather than interpretative. The reasons are twofold. First, computer generated reports are usually poorly laid out. Given that most computerised personnel systems offer limited report formatting (although this is improving rapidly with the next generation of MS-Windows-based software), it is worthwhile considering transferring the data into more flexible reporting tools (wordprocessing, graphics and spreadsheet packages). These proprietary packages are cheap and easy to use, so a small investment in training can reap major benefits). A second but important point is that different internal clients require different degrees of detail, different formats and different frequency of report. The example of absence monitoring, opposite, illustrates the point.

Figures 2.1 and 2.2 summarise the requirement for an effective absence management programme and demonstrate a typical format.

The internal clients can, therefore, be categorised and each will have their own demands. The effective HR function needs to quantify these against the following criteria:

- What information/service do we provide today?
- What do they need?
- What will it take to meet this requirement in terms of time, money and effort?

It is unlikely that you will be able to meet all the demands, so some degree of compromise is inevitable and this means prioritisation. Provided that the prioritisation is well argued in terms of the overall business and operational need, these

Absence monitoring and reporting

Senior executives. Directors and departmental heads are interested in overall levels, the trends, reason for variance and the cost. They prefer data to be presented in graph form, thereby showing at a glance whether their particular function has improved or worsened. Cost is key. If possible all HR reports should translate a trend/activity into monetary cost. This will guarantee readership.

Line managers. Too often personnel has demanded that line managers complete forms and procedures that have no obvious benefit to them. They, too, need relevant reports or ones which provide comparative data against other sections or departments. And while they, too, need graphs which highlight movements and comparative levels with other sections, they also need the detail of individual absence records so that they can review and, where necessary, take appropriate action.

Supervisors/employees. At this level, supervisors and individual employees often try to use Personnel to deflect responsibility. Issues become a 'personal problem' rather than a management question. This can become a waste of valuable resources and is certainly a poor substitute for good management. Both require sight of the attendance calendar to highlight the pattern and incidence of individual absence.

demands should be summarised as key objectives for the department.

Such action has the benefit of public focus and will help manage expectations. If any particular group feels a given

Figure 2.1
Absence monitoring pack

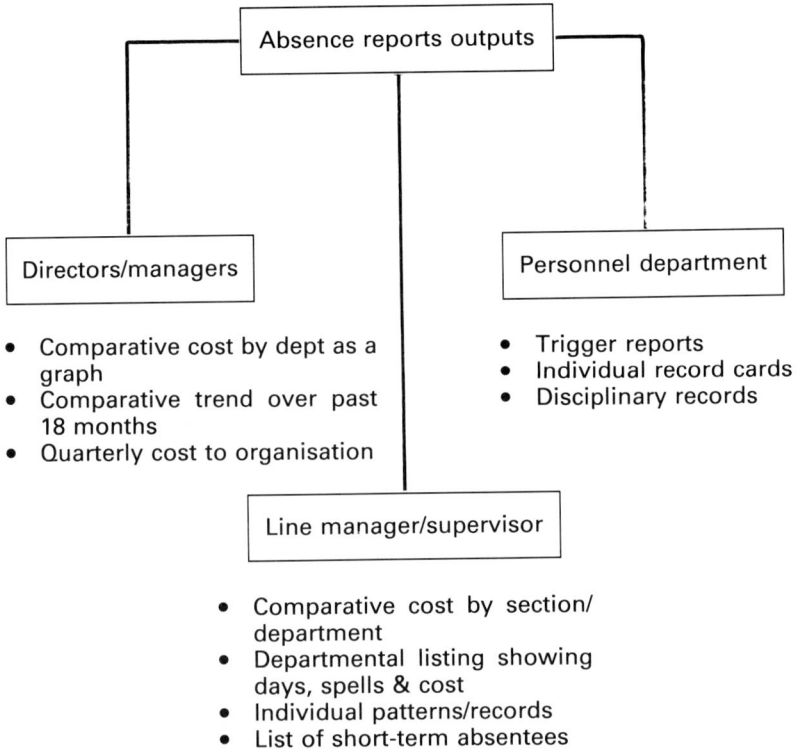

```
                    ┌─────────────────────────────┐
          ┌─────────┤   Absence reports outputs   ├─────────┐
          │         └──────────────┬──────────────┘         │
          │                        │                        │
          │                        │                        │
┌─────────┴──────────┐             │          ┌─────────────┴─────────┐
│ Directors/managers │             │          │ Personnel department  │
└────────────────────┘             │          └───────────────────────┘
                                    │
```

- Comparative cost by dept as a graph
- Comparative trend over past 18 months
- Quarterly cost to organisation

- Trigger reports
- Individual record cards
- Disciplinary records

```
                    ┌─────────────────────────────┐
                    │  Line manager/supervisor    │
                    └─────────────────────────────┘
```

- Comparative cost by section/department
- Departmental listing showing days, spells & cost
- Individual patterns/records
- List of short-term absentees

Reproduced with the permission of HR-BC Ltd

activity should be included or re-prioritised, this will need to be argued and justified against other declared interests or, alternatively, accommodated through provision of additional resources.

An HR audit, consequently, helps identify competing pressures for resource and through its customer focus will help clarify the business priorities. Measurement of both current activity and future requirement, therefore, establishes the parameters of, and realistic targets for, the department.

So for all those chief executives who have declared that

Figure 2.2

Quarterly comparison of absence rates: UK manufacturing company

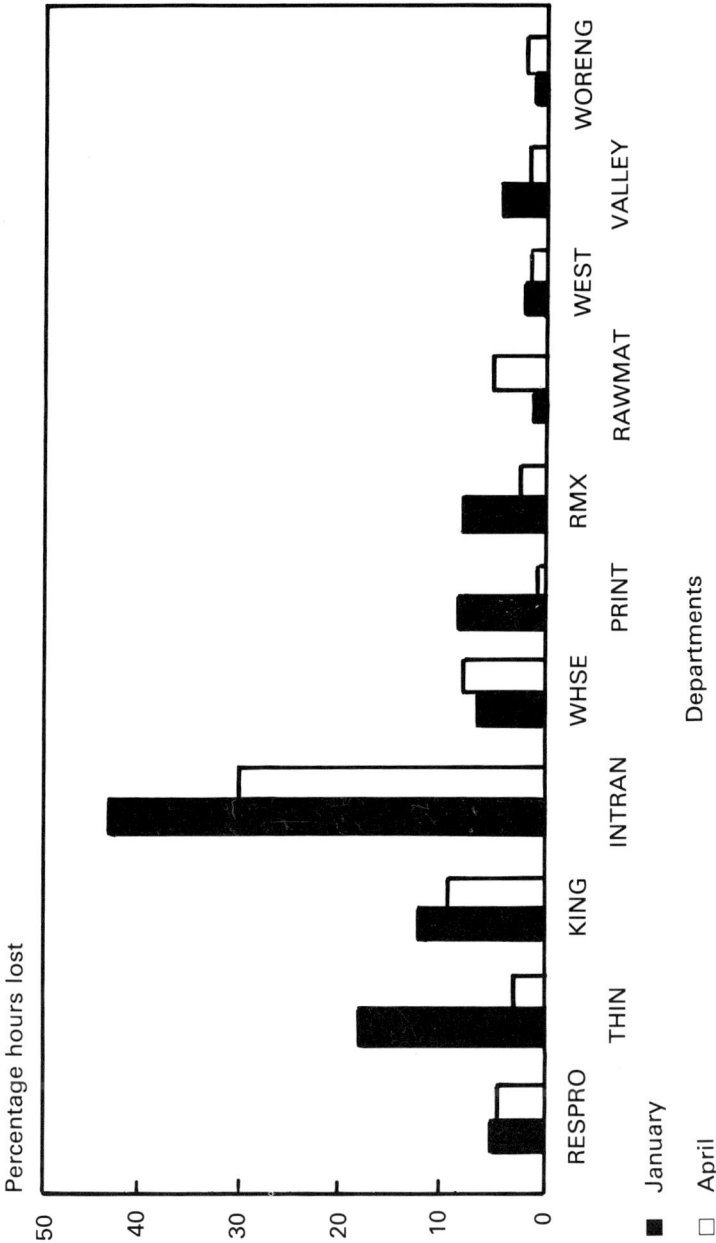

Figure 2.2

'people are our greatest asset', HR measurement can help demonstrate the commitment and the function gains credibility by joining the legion who subscribe to the philosophy 'if you can't measure it, you can't manage it'. But there are other significant benefits:

- *For the department*. Measurement of HR activity will provide clarity and focus of purpose; organisational credibility; pride and improved morale as staff know what is expected of them and how the service is received; plus a goal to aim for through specific targets of performance.
- *For the organisation*. Measurement will ensure that personnel practice becomes more closely aligned to business requirements, with better qualitative use of time, available budget and resources.

At Kent County Council, HR effectiveness was well defined as follows:

> Performance requirement is defined as what we have to do, need to do or want to do. Operational capability is how we're doing, how we find out how we are doing, and how we are going to improve.
>   This has been achieved by adopting three management principles:
>
> (1)   Stay close to the customer.
> (2)   Management not administration.
> (3)   Devolved accountability.

Within the Council the creation of an 'internal market' has been reflected by splitting corporate and support costs. The latter have to be negotiated and agreed through Service Level Agreements. The client also has the choice of looking elsewhere (to the private sector for example). The result has been that central support/service departments have become smaller, highly accountable, better-managed, customer-focused units.

Staff within these units are now more professional, more focused and more satisfied.

Looking for quick wins

As many companies and public sector organisations have now recognised, change is vital. But change is designed for one principal purpose – to improve the service provided to the customer. In practice it is far easier to improve the value of the personnel function to your organisation through lots of small gains than a high risk 'big bang'.

This point was also made by Alan Fowler, who in 1987 rightly observed that 'value for money should not be pursued as an end in itself. Personnel needs to find a justifiable balance between providing a good service or reaching a good decision quickly or economically, rather than searching for the ideal or perfect decision with expense and delay'.[1] Critical to this argument is that the function must be able to defend its decision with reference to supporting evidence.

To win recognition Personnel has to show it has made progress towards providing a quality effective service and to do this it needs priorities, clear performance targets, monitoring *and* celebration. Personnel needs to create a success culture.

References

1   Alan Fowler, 'What is the Value of Personnel Departments?', *Local Government Chronicle*, No. 6246, March 1987.

3

Conducting an HR Audit

The aim of a human resource audit is to provide a systematic examination of the department's activities. It looks to review objectively personnel policy, procedure and practice against planned or expected results.

The audit needs to be undertaken as a proactive, creative exercise with open participation by members of the function plus a representative sample of Personnel's internal clients. It cannot be imposed but must be seen to have senior management backing (so results and recommendations will be taken seriously).

Some will naturally view an audit with suspicion. Audits are usually undertaken from financial perspectives and in the current climate might easily be associated with job reductions. An alternative line needs to be offered. This should emphasise that an HR audit is an essential step towards improving departmental credibility and overall quality goals. It is, therefore, a check on compliance with legislative and company procedures.

Scope of the audit

The audit should cover three areas:

- Identifying current procedure and practice
- Analysing cost and the effectiveness of time and resource allocation
- Reviewing clients' satisfaction and expectations.

It will help to highlight both the function's strengths and weaknesses and thus will identify areas for improvement, and help to define service standards.

26

The HR audit should have three aspects:

- *Systems audit.* This reviews the paperflow, the procedures, and the controls. It includes all forms, records and files, whether held manually or on computer.
- *Operations audit.* This reviews how efficiently these systems are applied in practice. For example, how well people use given forms, how effective are reports and the costs involved.
- *Climate audit.* This reviews what people think of the function and compares this against Personnel's own perceptions.

In addition, the audit needs to take account of special focus areas. These might be wider corporate initiatives or the use of third-party services (e.g. consultancy, external training provision or subcontracted services).

Setting up the audit

The review can be designed internally or by using external consultants. Both have some advantages and disadvantages.

An internal exercise should be undertaken by an individual from outside the function. While the person may already have detailed knowledge of the company, this needs to be balanced against the advantage of untainted objective review. There may also be issues of authority, since the individual needs to have sufficient respect to question staff of differing levels of seniority. Also, people are less likely to be candid to a fellow employee.

Using external consultants has the following general advantages:

- Independent, improved objectivity
- Experience in other organisations: potential comparisons

- Professional authority
- Shorter time for completion.

The caveat is that any audit needs to be tailored to each organisation (a pre-set format can test elements of good practice but will not necessarily measure satisfaction or expectations sufficiently). It must also give value for money. Any report must clearly identify areas for improvement and propose how these can be achieved given resource or budget constraints.

Depending on the size of the organisation and the number of locations to be reviewed, an external consultant would normally expect an audit to take between two or three days on site, plus a further day of report writing and presentation. Clearly an internal exercise would take similar time but would also need additional time for preparation and set up.

First stage

The audit requires the following base data:

- Summary of corporate business goals
- Overview of organisation structure
- Details of company-wide initiatives.

Second stage

To review personnel activity, the audit requires:

- A statement of personnel's objectives
- Structure of the personnel department
- Copies of all standard personnel administration
- List and examples of HR management reports
- Copies of personnel policies
- Review of employee personal files
- Skills audit of personnel team

- IT/personnel systems review
- Cost/time analysis.

Third stage

To judge the effectiveness of the service, the review should include structured interviews with a selection of the department's clients:

- Looking at the interface with personnel
- A check on the understanding of the role
- A satisfaction review
- Review of needs/expectations
- Comment on communication policy.

Fourth stage

In documenting the findings, the audit report needs to address a number of additional points:

- A rating index against HR standards
- A rating index on satisfaction
- Summary of cost/time analysis
- Risk analysis identifying potential ability to cater for a major crisis and ability to accommodate change
- Identification of the Quality Gap (areas for improvement) and recommendations to close the gap
- The means to monitor progress.

Business understanding

If one of the key objectives for Personnel is to get closer to business and operational management, it needs to ensure that it fully understands corporate and operational short- and medium-term aims. Too often senior personnel staff cannot summarise these; furthermore, everybody in the department needs to be aware.

Frequently there is a clash of priorities and poor timing. We recommend that Personnel should try to match its own calendar of priorities against known corporate events. This will highlight potential pressures. A recent example involved a major electronics company which was planning to introduce a new shift system in October 1992. This was also the time when personnel were planning to launch a new appraisal scheme. Not only would these major initiatives impact strongly on the limited personnel resources but, since both demanded line management commitment, the appraisal implementation was virtually doomed. Figures 3.1, 3.2 and 3.3 illustrate how this might have been identified in advance.

Clear personnel objectives

The function needs to have clear stated objectives and priorities for the forthcoming year and the medium term (three to five years). These should be explicit and include realistic targets. They need to be agreed with the senior management team, agreed with the personnel team, and then documented and published.

Steve Connock has provided excellent guidance in his book *HR Vision*, which I recommend to all. Crucial to HR effectiveness is clarity and focus in these objectives. Connock stresses the need for:

- Alignment of HR vision to business strategies
- Publication of Personnel's 'manifesto'
- A vision of the future – Personnel needs to provide a picture of what the function will be providing in two or three years' time
- A statement of HR management principles

Figure 3.1
Example business calendar

	Jan	Feb	Mar
Qtr 1	Sales and marketing recruitment	Company audit 1992 budget deadline	Budget! New advertising campaign
	Apr	May	Jun
Qtr 2	Financial year start	New product launch	Total Quality Mgt launch Annual General Meeting
	Jul	Aug	Sep
Qtr 3	Senior management conference	Maintenance shut down	European office launch (Berlin)
	Oct	Nov	Dec
Qtr 4	New production shift introduced (Manchester/ Leeds)	R & D plan presented	Budget results

- A map of progression or development, illustrating where the function is now and how it needs to change for the future.

In essence the objectives should be the equivalent of the personnel department's mission statement. Publication probably needs to be at two levels:

1 *Strategic* – to dovetail into corporate business plans.
2 *Operational* – to enable personnel staff and line managers to understand immediate performance targets.

Our experience has shown that the majority of personnel staff

Figure 3.2
Example Group Personnel calendar

	Jan	Feb	Mar
Qtr 1	Personnel budgets prepared	Graduate milk round commences	Private health renewals Quarterly stats
	Apr	**May**	**Jun**
Qtr 2	1st salary models Schedules for managers	Revised costings	Salary review implemented Quarterly stats
	Jul	**Aug**	**Sep**
Qtr 3	Company personnel conference		Quarterly stats Graduate trainee programme starts Car fleet policy agreed
	Oct	**Nov**	**Dec**
Qtr 4	Appraisals undertaken – IPM Conference	Annual Report preparation	Annual stats

and clients cannot describe the role or objectives of the function. This may be because the departments have no mission statements, or plans may exist but are not adequately disseminated.

A leading company, for example, had briefed its personnel section with the following objectives for 1993:

- To concentrate on activities as a business function not on administration or welfare
- To concentrate on areas of competitive advantage
- Training and development linked to NVQs
- Restructuring
- Cost reduction.

Figure 3.3

Example combined business/Personnel calendar

	Jan	Feb	Mar
Qtr 1	Sales and marketing recruitment - - - - - - - - - - - - - - - Personnel budget prepared	Company audit Budget deadlines - - - - - - - - - - - - - - - Graduate milk round commences	New budgets agreed New advertising campaign - - - - - - - - - - - - - - - Private health renewals Quarterly stats
	Apr	**May**	**Jun**
Qtr 2	Financial year start - - - - - - - - - - - - - - - Salary review starts Salary model prepared Schedules for managers	New product launch - - - - - - - - - - - - - - - Revised costings	Total Quality Mgt launch Annual General Meeting - - - - - - - - - - - - - - - Salary review implemented Quarterly stats
	Jul	**Aug**	**Sep**
Qtr 3	Senior Mgt Conference - - - - - - - - - - - - - - - Company personnel conference	Maintenance shut down - - - - - - - - - - - - - - -	European office launch (Berlin) - - - - - - - - - - - - - - - Graduate trainee Car fleet policy issue Quarterly stats
	Oct	**Nov**	**Dec**
Qtr 4	New production shift introduced (Manchester/Leeds) - - - - - - - - - - - - - - - Appraisal programme start IPM Conference	R & D plan - - - - - - - - - - - - - - - Annual report preparation	Corporate budget review - - - - - - - - - - - - - - - Annual stats

These were not documented. A number of the personnel staff
had not been able to attend the meeting and only one could
remember these objectives six months on. Line managers
found it difficult to describe Personnel's role.

Furthermore, the department was identified as being
forward-thinking in terms of training and development programmes but bureaucratic, obstructive and conservative in
day-to-day administration. In fact the majority of the team
largely focused on welfare and administrative tasks – in
complete contrast to the first stated objective. None of the
objectives had time or performance criteria.

Reviewing practice and procedure

Under HR-BC's *Quality in Personnel Practice* (*QIPP*) programme, personnel practice and procedures are examined
under the following ten broad categories of activities:

- Human resource strategy and planning
- Recruitment and selection
- Personnel records
- Salaries and remuneration
- Performance appraisal
- Absence policy
- Establishment/post control
- Training and development
- Employee relations
- Departmental administration.

For each category, the audit checks actual activity against
accepted best practice (as demonstrated by leading organisations, IPM codes of practice, UK and EC statutes and
regulations). For example, most organisations will have a
written statement that they are an 'equal opportunity

employer' but what evidence is there of the policy being monitored in practice?

- Does the equal opportunity policy cover recruitment, promotions, training and development, remuneration and appraisal?
- Is an equal opportunity log maintained at each stage of the recruitment process?
- Is a disability register maintained?
- Is there a special policy to assist disabled people, e.g. adaptations in the workplace?
- Has the organisation set specific equal opportunity targets, e.g. in terms of ethnic minority recruitment, women managers, training provision?
- What equal opportunity reports are generated? At what frequency? And with what impact?

The audit needs to cover every area of personnel practice, for example:

- Sickness absence
- Maternity leave
- Holiday procedures
- Grievance
- Disciplinary procedures
- Job specification
- Recruitment advertising
- Selection testing
- Personal records
- Termination procedures
- Staff movements
- Data protection
- Remuneration
- Pension administration
- Performance management
- Training and development
- Organisation charts
- Succession planning
- Career planning
- Job evaluation
- Competency/skill profiling.

Cost and time analysis

Rarely do personnel functions analyse how and where they allocate resources in terms of people, time and money. It is essential they do so in a management climate where all resources are under scrutiny.

One way is to ask each member of the team to list the main activities their job involves – most will provide between five and eight – and then to approximate the percentage amount of time they spend on each.

This is guaranteed to be most revealing. It serves two purposes: first, the totals can be aggregated to give a good idea of where the department spends its time; second, it provides a reality check of what is actually done compared with the department goals (see above). Two examples of personal time analysis are given below.

Personnel administrator	%
1 Recruitment	25
2 Updating personal records	15
3 Share save scheme	5
4 Maternity leave	10
5 Absence monitoring	20
6 *Ad hoc* reports	25

Employee relations manager	%
1 Manpower reviews	15
2 Union negotiations	20
3 Policy review	20
4 Management meetings	15
5 Disciplinary hearing	10
6 Grievance	5
7 Job evaluation	15

A typical aggregate of time spent by the whole personnel department is illustrated in Figure 3.4.

Figure 3.4
Time analysis of a personnel department:
UK engineering group

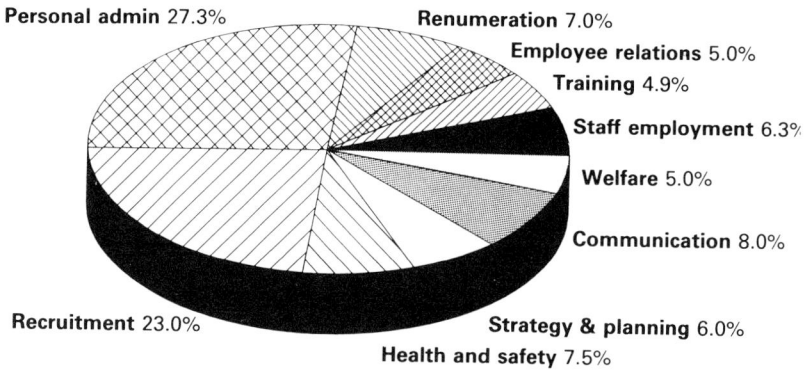

Personal admin 27.3%

Renumeration 7.0%

Employee relations 5.0%

Training 4.9%

Staff employment 6.3%

Welfare 5.0%

Communication 8.0%

Recruitment 23.0%

Strategy & planning 6.0%

Health and safety 7.5%

This base data can now be usefully compared against:

1 *Budget allocation*. Does the time spent on key activities match both the aims and planned budget allocation?
2 *Client expectations*. Does the time spent on these activities match client requirements and expectation?
3 *Planning change*. To what degree does the department create time for analysis, change and implementation?

Analysing departmental costs

The audit should try to identify the departmental spend under given cost categories. Typical requests for data are as follows:

- Personnel staff salaries
- Personnel staff benefits
- Day-to-day running costs of the department

- Secretarial support
- IT budget (software purchase, support, hardware)
- Training and development
- Literature/market research (e.g. surveys)
- Consultancy/professional support
- Miscellaneous.

To be thorough, the review needs to distinguish costs which are internal to the function; those which are external but directly linked to Personnel; and those which can be associated with the impact of human resource management across the organisation as a whole.

Personnel skills

In addition to analysing time and activity, the audit needs to review the people and skills within the department. Four areas should be considered:

- Current skills
- Competency
- Stability (Personnel needs to consider likely turnover and the impact if it occurs)
- Motivation.

Use of information technology

This a crucial area. If computer systems are used, the department would benefit from a review of:

- *Objectives*. Whether the software is matching the original purchase objectives. If not, why?

- *Data audit.* How accurate is the data? Is it relevant? Is it used?
- *Reports.* What reports are generated from the software? For whom, at what frequency and in what format?
- *Knowledge.* To what degree is knowledge of the systems concentrated or shared among the department's staff? Is there back up should a person fall ill or leave?
- *Hardware layout.* Is this most effective? Can everybody access the software? Can they print reports easily?
- *Support.* How good is the suppliers' support? Do they give value for money? What internal support is required?
- *Integration.* Has the department made full use of its software? Do members of the department need training in the use of word processing, spreadsheets or graphics?

Measuring client satisfaction

It is impossible to use just one measure to assess the various clients' satisfaction with personnel activity. So a range of measures are more appropriate. The audit should try to distinguish client reactions in terms of:

- Relevance and importance
- Speed of response
- Quality of service.

In addition, it is useful to review how others view Personnel and check this against the function's own perceptions. These can be gleaned through structured interviews with staff within the department, senior executives/operational managers, line managers and team leaders.

The first important check is to see whether the clients share the same priorities and objectives. These should be broadly in line, although one of Personnel's key roles is to act as a check against unfair or unethical treatment. Some line managers might wish to be rid of all personnel procedure in dealing with hiring and firing, for example, where in their view personnel's professional responsibility may restrict or delay immediate reaction. The function needs to ensure that this important role is both understood and recognised.

The second check is of relevance and usefulness. Here clients should be asked to assess against a simple scale whether the forms, procedures and reports supplied meet basic criteria:

- Easy to use
- Easy to read/assimilate
- Provide limited/sufficient/too much information.

In essence, do they assist operational management or are they a burden? How could they be designed to be more appropriate?

The third check is of responsiveness. To what extent is Personnel both available and effective in responding? The case study featuring **KLM Royal Dutch Airlines** (see Chapter 6) highlights the ability of the department to meet 90 per cent of all line manager requests within five minutes. I have talked to many internal clients who complain that two to three weeks would be typical in their organisation. Speedy response is vital for credibility. If the department fails to be an information provider, clients will do their own thing and this is dangerous in terms of both maintaining a consistent approach and monitoring overall trends.

Quality is fundamental. Information provided needs to be accurate and authoritative. Credibility is rapidly undermined by incorrect data, inconsistent trends or variance. Many a department has suffered because of sets of figures that have been produced in too much haste without sufficient checking. The wrong headcount, a miscalculated salary model, inaccurate turnover figures – all are easily spotted. Personnel needs to ensure that any data provided has authority – given the cost of the paybill to the organisation any figures are likely to be significant and subject to the closest scrutiny. Once credibility is lost, it takes considerable effort and time to recover.

Reviewing clients' perception of the function is very revealing. Often those who use the department least or have the lowest contact will rate the function the highest in terms of professionalism, response, communication and openness. This was exemplified by one payroll manager who stated that Personnel must be efficient and effective because nobody ever talked about it!

HR-BC use a range of attributes (with two broad opposites) and ask internal clients to rate whether the function reflects a given or opposite attribute. This provides an individual map reflecting the culture of the department which, if undertaken with a sufficient number of internal clients, can be aggregated. Often clients will state that individual personalities have a significant impact, i.e. one individual is considered forward-thinking while others are seen as obstructive and conservative. To some degree this may be inevitable but it may also indicate that the function is giving off inconsistent signals. Equally some will state that personnel policy and practice is short term in outlook, while senior personnel staff claim more effort is being spent on becoming strategic.

Comment and criticism are important measures as they reflect 'perceived value'. We have stated that Personnel needs to demonstrate value to the organisation. It therefore needs to get this feedback and *be seen to react to it*. This form of review also avoids the danger of simply documenting procedures and practice without analysing operational results.

To satisfy clients, the department needs to ensure that it understands what its clients *want*. If there are problems, the proactive function will review and jointly resolve the issue rather than seek to justify why there are problems. By reviewing clients' satisfaction of Personnel, the department can start to focus on the areas for improvement – these will be those areas identified as high importance but low satisfaction.

In the final analysis, if a department is not doing what the organisation and its internal clients want, what is it doing?

Client needs

The second area of investigation involving internal clients is to examine their current requirements and likely future needs. This will help personnel gauge the scope, scale and rate of change necessary. For each stated requirement the audit should check adequacy of present practice, necessary change and how the department would meet the new requirement.

Client needs can be categorised into:

- Essential
- Necessary
- Desirable
- Undefined.

This will help prioritise areas for change or improvement.

Risk analysis

As the ICL case study indicates (see Chapter 5) an important criterion for Personnel is its ability both to respond to change and to help facilitate the business to change. Therefore, the audit should be able to assess the degree of flexibility and preparedness in given situations, for example:

- A major redundancy announcement
- A serious industrial relations dispute
- A major fire/industrial accident
- A take-over announcement or international merger
- Introduction of new legislation.

Benchmarking

Collating data is one thing, but it must be used to form the basis of an action plan. The information needs to be translated into reference points or *benchmarks* for performance or service standards.

These benchmarks become the starting points for measuring improvements, trends and movements in personnel activity. They must also have a time frame: some areas, e.g. absence control, might require weekly monitoring but not later than monthly if it is to be operationally effective; others might require monthly or quarterly review, e.g. recruitment, paybill monitoring or equal opportunities. If the time period set is too long, Personnel and managers alike will find that the data is outdated, preventing effective action to be taken to correct adverse trends or variances.

If analysis is only undertaken once a year or less, it is likely to be of marginal value and thus produced simply for presentation purposes. Ideally, performance targets should be set quarterly but monitored monthly.

Examples of performance ratios include:

- Average training cost per employee
- Average number of delegate days trained per quarter
- Average per capita cost of recruitment
- Percentage of vacancies filled before recruit-by date
- Percentage of enquiries responded to within 10 minutes
- Percentage of appraisals completed and logged by given date
- Monthly performance against HR budget
- Monthly equal opportunity analysis against
  - recruitment target
  - training opportunities.

Whatever measures are adopted, they must be seen as indicators and prompts for action – this is why trends and variances are more important than the figure itself. Secondly, targets need to be realistic but challenging. Ideally reports should be simple, graphical, published and used.

We would recommend that each main policy area should be reviewed quarterly. We also recommend that responsibility for these areas should be evenly distributed among the team so everybody has an area to monitor. A good example of shared accountability is illustrated in the KLM case study (see Chapter 6).

As described in Chapter 4, quality programmes demand a formal audit at least once every six months.

External comparisons

There have been recent articles which have published external comparisons measuring, for example:

- The number of personnel staff as a ratio to total headcount
- Personnel salary costs as a proportion of the total company paybill
- Comparative figures showing the costs of recruitment or training.

I would suggest that these figures must be treated with extreme caution. The figures tend to be aggregates across a wide variety of business sectors, differing sizes of organisation, and often have a relatively small survey base. In such cases, a 'national' average per capita cost of recruitment does not reflect the marked variance between those companies which make use of headhunters, agencies or run different advertising campaigns.

Such general comparative figures are of casual interest, but some practitioners are looking to use them to justify resources; they can be equally dangerous in the hands of cost-cutting chief executives. On the other hand there is a need to benchmark activities – against best practice in terms of recommended IPM, ITD or ACAS codes, for example, or indeed against the personnel practice of leading organisations both within your own sector and business generally. Here the function needs to review:

- What are the differences between current policies and recommended best practice?
- Why is Personnel in other organisations seen to be more (or less) effective?
- How could these differences be applied in your organisation?

SWOT analysis

All this information can then be summarised into a simple Strengths, Weaknesses, Opportunities and Threats grid, an example of which is shown in Figure 3.5. This may highlight the need for new skills, a change of emphasis or new ideas.

It does, however, ensure that the department has a good overall view of its performance and what it needs to do. This

Figure 3.5
Example SWOT grid for Personnel

STRENGTHS

- Defined recruitment processes
- Industrial relations advice
- Computerised personnel system
- Availability
- Equal opps monitoring
- Good manual records

OPPORTUNITIES

- Devolve day-to-day personnel operations
  - absence
  - disciplinary etc
- Reduce bureaucracy
- Training and skill development
- Investors in People
- Become more strategic
- Improve information
- Use IT more effectively

WEAKNESSES

- Lack of payroll integration
- Poor training records
- Poor quality reports
- Too operational
- No board representation
- Poor analysis e.g. absence

THREATS

- Line managers' own systems
- Inconsistent HR application
- Industrial tribunal cases
- Cuts in personnel staff
- Use of external consultants

can be described as the *Quality Gap*. The more it is able to anticipate change and prepare in advance, the better its response will be.

For each major heading identified under the HR-BC *QIPP* programme (see p. 34) the analysis will show how the department is reacting now, what is needed for the future and what is needed to get there – thus setting the agenda for HR development.

Once the initial report is completed, follow-up and feedback is required. Future reports, therefore, need to assess the status of any initial recommendations. They should be tabled as being fully met, partially completed or still outstanding.

Is it worthwhile?

Conducting an HR audit is the first crucial step in improving the service of the function. It collects facts and evidence of what you actually do and identifies what you need to do. Without these facts there can be no control, no defined standards of service and, thus, variable quality.

The audit also helps the department to clarify its role and sets out the priorities for action. It is impossible to improve everything in one step. By analysing the costs, identifying where resources are placed and defining the needs, the department can assess which actions will lead to most benefit in terms of improved value to the organisation.

The audit is also dynamic – it cannot be viewed as a one-off exercise. Circumstances will change, the organisation's needs will be changing – thus the development of the HR policy and practice must be continually evolving and, to be effective, improving. To achieve this continuous improvement regular audits and monitoring of activity are required.

The HR audit is the first step towards the quality personnel function.

4

Creating a Quality Framework

A quality environment will create HR effectiveness since it will be geared to providing client satisfaction at least cost. But what is meant by quality? Even though many organisations have adopted quality initiatives and are BS 5750 or ISO 9000 registered firms, their personnel functions may have had only a minor involvement. This is surprising given that the personnel function is often charged with communicating quality programmes to the workforce.

One of the reasons is that these quality standards are primarily geared to the design, production and delivery of company products and services. On first reading, the standards would only seem to impact on Personnel in terms of training and training records – and these may have been devolved to the line anyway. More recently, however, a number of personnel functions have adopted quality programmes in order to improve (or justify) their contribution to the business and to be seen to be participating in wider initiatives. Some have been forced to as part of Total Quality Management (TQM) programmes.

What do we mean by quality?

Quality can be defined as meeting client requirements. By using this definition, quality can become the goal of every personnel department. It also demands consistent performance to agreed standards, which are monitored and updated, to guarantee reliability. Two other important criteria may be aesthetics (for example, that the HR reports are not only accurate but also look good and encourage people to want to use them), and 'perceived quality' – the service provided must be considered good value (i.e. it is affordable and contributes

47

to business profitability). In general terms this notion of quality is often described as 'fitness for purpose' or meeting stated and implied needs.

For our purposes this can be seen as ensuring personnel policies and practices are designed to meet business and legislative requirements and are delivered in the most cost-effective and efficient manner. This is why we are interested in improving the quality of Personnel. It sounds simple but in practice tends to be somewhat complex.

To meet client requirements implies that we have identified them; that we have discussed and understood what they want; and that we have become truly client-oriented, i.e. we have focused all our activities to meeting these needs. This means getting much closer to the line, with more hands-on activity – if we spend all our time cocooned in personnel offices, how can we ever satisfy our clients? In addition, personnel policy and practice must be seen as an aid not a hindrance.

As internal clients have differing requirements, so there may be a range of personnel activity and it will need to be flexible. It is also dynamic. We must be seen as innovative and forward-thinking, and the various systems we introduce and recommend have to accommodate change.

Too often in the past, job evaluation schemes or payment structures were constructed as control mechanisms. In many organisations these systems now have become barriers to change. In my experience most personnel functions will need to take a major step – change in culture – to meet these challenges. A quality improvement programme can provide the means to achieve this goal.

What is a quality framework?

A quality framework establishes a structure for the various processes and systems used by Personnel to get the tasks done. It includes HR strategy and planning since it must be proactive, looking to anticipate change, and preventing and alleviating problems or issues.

Research by those responsible for introducing and monitoring wider quality programmes has shown that the majority of errors arise because people did not fully understand what to do; they lacked the correct information or tools to complete the task. The procedural framework must therefore be comprehensive but, most important of all, it needs to be simple and *used*. If a quality framework is not used, it can hardly be described as a quality procedure nor can it be effective. The framework we should be seeking, therefore, does not need to be the best but it must be understood by everybody and be used by them.

Some have described establishing the quality framework as maximising client satisfaction. In this way Personnel should not aim simply to meet the demands of line managers, senior executives, employees and applicants, but should wish to delight them.

Is it affordable?

In the past the personnel function has suffered through poor presentation, bureaucratic administration and lack of influence. As a consequence it has found resources and budgets limited; and, while keen to be more proactive, Personnel sometimes lacks the courage to pursue such a demanding cultural change. Here are some reasons why you cannot afford to miss the opportunity.

First, the department cannot stay still – the process of change is now an accepted part of the business environment. The function must adapt. If it does not, the line will take over the activities or demand that they be met by others, since the department's service will be valued less and less.

Second, the activities will need to be provided with least cost, which demands a continual review of effectiveness. This will ensure that there is a means of improving and taking advantage of technical and managerial innovation. Providing service with least cost does not just mean being efficient, it also requires that personnel is effective by being efficient in the right areas. To do so the function must prioritise its resources.

Third, 'quality has always made people rich', claimed Tom Peters, the co-author of *In Search of Excellence*. Quality service, even from the personnel function, leads to respect and more demand from the internal client. This in turn enables the function to grow. In the same way, poor quality or poor performance will lead to a rapid decline in demand.

Fourth, it's what your internal clients want. If you fail to provide what they want, the quality gap – i.e. the difference between what you actually provide and their expectations – will widen.

Fifth, it is a great motivator – personnel staff like to take pride in their work as much as anyone else. If this is appreciated and respected, their job satisfaction will grow markedly. They will seek out new challenges. The quality framework helps because it not only provides the focus on the internal client but it also encourages greater teamwork and co-operation, so everyone has a valued contribution. In addition, quality demands accountability and responsibility. But most important of all it creates a challenge. As a result, a quality improvement programme within the personnel function will unite the team by providing clear goals and targets.

Sixth, a quality initiative looks at improvement – it concentrates on effectiveness and it provides a vehicle for the personnel director/manager to establish true leadership of the team.

These seem to be six very good reasons for championing such a programme. But what is the alternative? No one wants to head up or even work in a team that is characterised by:

- *Complaints* about the speed of response and poor quality of the data provided.
- *Frustration* of wasted time checking up on details or duplicating data entry in manual and computer formats.

- *Confusion* because you seem to be the last to know, often creating embarrassment.
- *Firefighting* from one melodrama to the next because people do not follow the written procedures.
- *Overwork* with so much to do that it impacts on your leisure.

Yet most of us have done it – and, from my experience, a large number of personnel departments are still there today.

These make compelling practitioner-oriented reasons why we need to seek change. But there are even stronger reasons for the organisation. If personnel practice and procedure is not consistently followed (because it is unclear, unread and considered of low relevance to operational management), there will be inequitable and inconsistent behaviour by line managers. The result will be potential legal claims, higher turnover, rising absenteeism, uncontrolled recruitment cost, bias in appraisal, plus inflated and contentious remuneration. Together these are likely to amount to costs of £1m to £2m per year for an organisation of some 500 employees.

Commitment

The crucial element of success is commitment: a desire to change. This needs to come from all levels. Some people talk of commitment from the top. This is fundamental – the personnel function needs backing from the chief executive and other operational directors for the programme and this must be obtained at board level. But you should get it – after all, senior executives are likely to back a programme which helps line management in meeting the business needs and improves effectiveness. Most have been waiting for just such a proposal.

But success also needs commitment from your own team. Some quality initiatives have faltered because they were simply one person's vision and not that of the employees. The change must involve everyone in the team and be achieved by the team. Otherwise quality will be imposed (e.g. by dictate that all functions must document all processes and procedures to meet BS 5750 standards). Expressed in this way it becomes an unwelcome chore on top of the normal activities of the personnel department.

A quality framework establishes sound management practice. Applied to human resource management it will ensure that:

- Personnel policies are properly designed, implemented and monitored to show effectiveness, fairness and direction.
- The service (reports, advice and administration) assists line and operational managers to recruit the right people, train them correctly, retain and motivate them.
- Skills and potential are used to the full.
- Effective communication is established so that the organisation is able to move forward together. This means developing a climate of openness and trust, thereby enabling frank two-way feedback.

At Edmund Nuttall Ltd (see Chapter 9) the Human Resources Director sought the personal backing of the Chief Executive for the plan and obtained full board approval of the project. He then briefed his team and operational management about the aims. This was backed up by a regular weekly lunch-time briefing of the personnel staff to ensure everybody was able to participate and contribute to the quality improvement programme. In this way the quality framework was fuelled by the personnel staff and their motivation.

Commitment needs to be backed up by training since any improvement programme must be sustained. If you are contemplating a TQM or a BS 5750/ISO 9000 standard, this will be a necessity. Once registered, the organisation will be subject to regular surveillance visits. Losing certification would be potentially worse than not having achieved it in the first place.

The long-term nature of the programme is often under-estimated, hence the need for active participation. Resistance is rarely due to obstruction – in most cases programme fatigue develops because staff views and suggestions are not considered fully. HR audits and a quality framework give individuals, both inside the department and clients, the opportunity to have their say. Many people we interview cynically ask us whether Personnel will publish the results.

Combining HR goals, strategy and practice

It is impossible to deliver a quality service if you are not clear about the department's role and what is expected of it from senior executives and line managers alike. This demands a *vision*. The vision needs to state why the department exists, what is it going to provide and within what timescale. An example, in broad terms, is that personnel should aim:

> . . . *to provide a valued contribution through high-quality HR advice, policy and practice which enables the department's clients to meet their business plans.*

The vision needs to be translated into a *mission*. This should set out where the department is going, and how it is going to get there. For example:

> *By continually improving the service provided to ensure that internal client needs are met, that innovation and growth is encouraged and that the potential of employees is maximised to the full benefit of the organisation.*

The mission needs to be backed up by high-principled personnel *values*. Some have called these Critical Success Factors – in essence if we could meet a similar set of values the department would be viewed as effective. See the ICL HR standards reproduced in Chapter 5 (p. 89) for an example of such standards. Others might include:

- *HR strategy will be determined from agreed corporate business plans and will fully integrate with operational requirements.*
- *HR policies and practices will be clearly documented and effectively communicated.*
- *Standards of performance will be established for all HR activity, and monitored at least quarterly with explanation plus planned actions.*
- *The department will seek to adopt best HR practice in order to release the full potential of all employees.*

These statements can then be backed by specific short-term *targets* or objectives for the next 6 to 12 months. Targets may include:

- Achieve Investors in People accreditation by September 1994.
- Reduce absenteeism by two percentage points to an overall site level of 3.5 per cent.
- Ensure that every employee is appraised during 1993 and their progress is formally reviewed every six months.
- Ensure that every employee has a personal development plan agreed with their immediate manager.

To meet these targets, *processes* need to be designed, defined and communicated. These processes will cover the main activities or tasks undertaken. But note these activities not only include those within the department but should also cover the interface with the clients, i.e. line managers, employees, applicants and senior executives.

The role of the department as it moves towards provision of a quality service is illustrated in Figure 4.1.

One of the key elements which Personnel needs to address is linkage of HR strategy to both business strategy and IT strategy. We have already stressed the need for Personnel to

Figure 4.1
Combining strategy with procedure

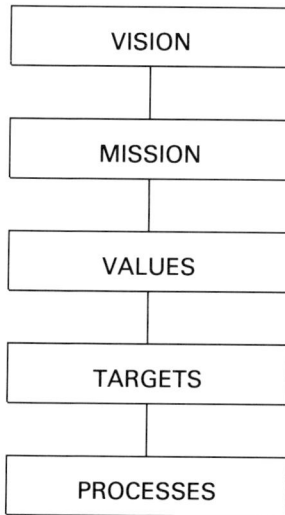

```
┌─────────────────────┐
│       VISION        │
└──────────┬──────────┘
           │
┌──────────┴──────────┐
│       MISSION       │
└──────────┬──────────┘
           │
┌──────────┴──────────┐
│       VALUES        │
└──────────┬──────────┘
           │
┌──────────┴──────────┐
│       TARGETS       │
└──────────┬──────────┘
           │
┌──────────┴──────────┐
│      PROCESSES      │
└─────────────────────┘
```

get closer to the business goals and the line. But IT has the greatest potential to implement change, and speedily.

Consultants Ernst & Young, for example, identified the following characteristics:

- Where business strategy and HR strategy were not closely co-ordinated, the board had often failed to communicate its business objectives; communications between depart-ments were poor; a lack of co-operation meant some departments blocked initiatives; and management hier-archies thrived.
- Where IT strategy and HR strategy were poorly linked, systems were typically of functional relevance only; of piecemeal development without supporting wider business goals; unreliable and often work-creating rather than ad-ministratively effective.

Yet where *all* three strategies were closely linked, organisations typically had very strong corporate values; were very flexible, innovative, and able to adapt and streamline operations effectively.

What is required of a quality system?

A quality system focuses on the management process – essentially *how* we do things rather than the end result – the principle being that if the procedures are well thought-out, well organised and well implemented they will achieve their aim. Personnel is often described as having bright ideas that never come to fruition: too often we have failed on implementation. Quality systems and their associated standards can help us to ensure that we take care to make certain our plans are successful. The programmes will still need amendment but we will have a better chance of reaching declared targets. In general terms, this is where BS 5750/ISO 9000 comes into play. These are the internationally recognised standards for such a quality system.

With so much cynicism about personnel activity and accusations of bureaucracy, Personnel needs quality systems urgently. But quality standards are not just rules; applied correctly they should ensure that problems do not recur, that procedures are adopted fairly and consistently, and that the team works as one.

Quality systems, including the BS 5750/ISO 9000 series, require formal documentation to ensure conformity, i.e. any person can read a given procedure to see what should be done.

Why do we need documentation?

We all loathe documentation – it is synonymous with bureaucracy. Forms for forms' sake! And this has been the problem with many corporate demands to seek BS 5750 registration. Staff are simply told, in the interests of BS 5750 (which means little to most people) and quality, to document everything they do to the nth degree. In most cases this becomes a chore and an unwelcome burden on top of everyday operational demands. People may start well but after a while fail to complete the task through what can only be described as 'programme fatigue'.

Yet documentation is crucial. For many organisations and personnel departments, the 'best way' or 'correct method' is in people's heads. It is not written down and they get by. This may be adequate in the short term, but what happens if the person is struck down by injury or illness or is offered a more lucrative position at the company across the road? There is no record. The successor simply brings his or her own style and interpretation. At this stage personnel policy and practice shows marked signs of inconsistency.

Consultants who undertake HR audits are often told 'it depends who you are dealing with' – i.e. personnel practice is based on personalities rather than effective, accepted norms. This is particularly true of larger companies and corporations who have pursued a policy of rotating junior and middle management in posts for two to three years as a way of providing experience. For those in the factories (who may have considerable length of service), personnel practice is viewed as being very personal and changeable. This is totally at odds with notions of quality. To be credible in a world where there has been increased delegation and empowerment of people management to the line, Personnel needs to be seen as a source of excellence. Indeed, it must take on the role of adviser or internal consultant. It can only succeed in this role if it has authority and is respected. This demands consistency and good practice – hence the need for documentation.

But this must be effective documentation *not* bureaucracy. How can we judge this distinction?

- First, the documentation must be available to anybody who needs it.
- Second, it must be precise, up-to-date, regularly reviewed and relevant.

- Third, it needs to be clear and unambiguous. It must be readable.
- Fourth, it must be an aid *not* an unwelcome control.

These are tough criteria. How many personnel procedures manuals or staff handbooks would score four out of four? Of the voluminous tomes I see, very few make easy reading. Most are *not* read – as line managers admit – and hardly any have guidance on how to use the procedures in practice (e.g. inclusion of illustrative examples). No wonder managers fall foul of the procedure. Worse still, many manuals are not reviewed and amended as a matter of course – once in print it becomes the company 'bible'. This cannot be the right approach in a changing world: we need to be flexible; procedures must adapt otherwise they become counterproductive.

We need, therefore, a means of documenting personnel practice which provides clarity, completeness and can allow rapid revision.

Flowcharting – a novel approach

Flowcharting is particularly effective for documenting personnel practice, as it matches the criteria set out above. But its real benefit is that it provides line management and the personnel team with a simple, clear and graphic summary of what action is required. A single chart can replace 12 pages of typed text; a personnel manual of over 40 pages can be translated into 15–20 pages, presented in a readily digestible format.

Unfortunately Personnel has tended to be wordy. It has taken a long time for practitioners to recognise the need to use graphics for impact. It has yet to be widely appreciated that graphs are not just for show but to illustrate variance or trends. This is where quality of management will be demonstrated through interpretation.

Equally in policy and procedure, Personnel's anxiety to ensure that all clauses are legally correct has made many a document difficult to read, let alone to comprehend. Flowcharts, however, give a visual summary. Furthermore, many operational managers will be used to the format; it is Personnel which may find the technique difficult to grasp in the first instance.

Flowcharts clarify the process (see Figure 4.2). They show order and the logical progression of decision-making towards a given outcome. This helps set expectations. Quality gurus like to talk of 'process management' to replace administrative routine (they claim a routine implies rigidity, red tape and legal technicalities).

Designing flowcharts also helps to identify duplication or bottlenecks. The chart represents a structured, step-by-step approach which links decisions with appropriate documents, forms or record systems. The framework therefore highlights the sequence of decision-making and the associated information/paperflow (see Figure 4.3). Both give the department considerable opportunity to examine the relevance of each stage or form and hence its 'fitness for purpose'. By doing so the function can review the efficiency and consistency of actions and, consequently, its effectiveness in key activities.

The resulting manual is not only attractive and innovative, it is also much easier to use – and, therefore, more likely to be used. Consequently, flowcharting provides a means whereby a quality initiative within the function gives a practical, tangible end-result of real value to the business, not just a document for the sake of documenting what we do.

Translating quality into personnel practice

The key role of Personnel is to maximise employees' potential to the benefit of the organisation – in effect to develop the organisation. This has been recognised by the Personnel

Figure 4.2
Flowchart illustration of a training procedure

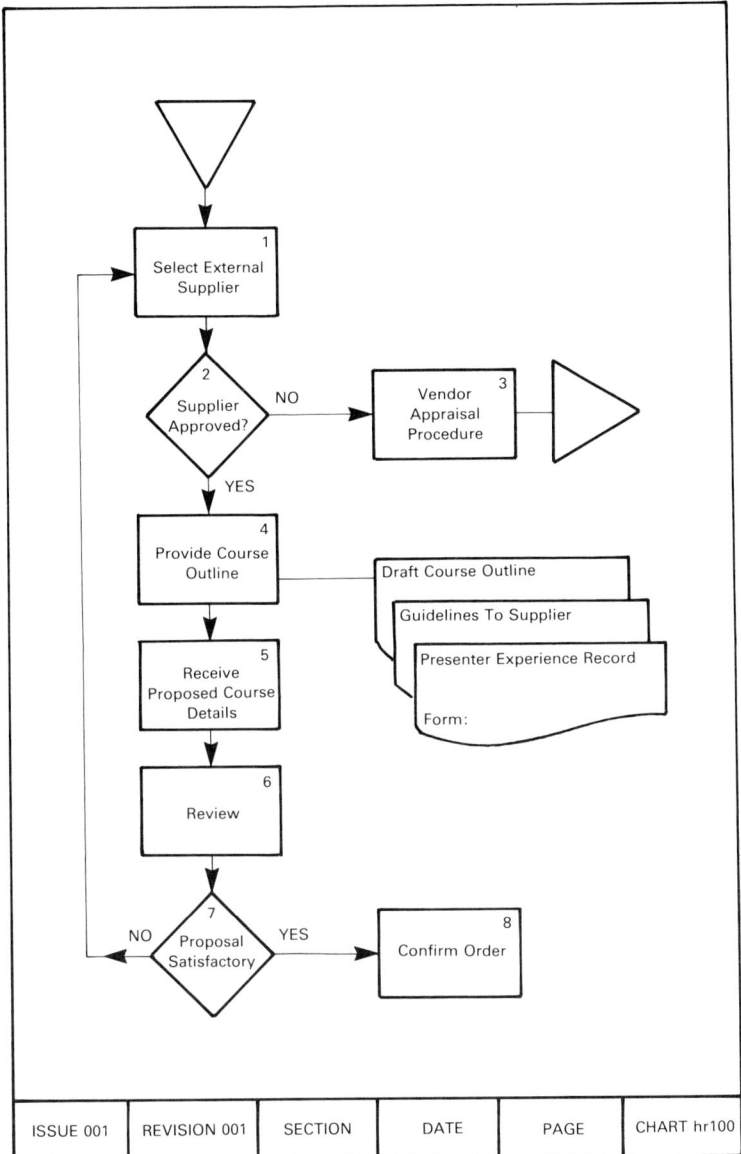

ISSUE 001	REVISION 001	SECTION	DATE	PAGE	CHART hr100

Reproduced with the permission of HR-BC Ltd

Figure 4.3
Flowchart illustration of staff recruitment

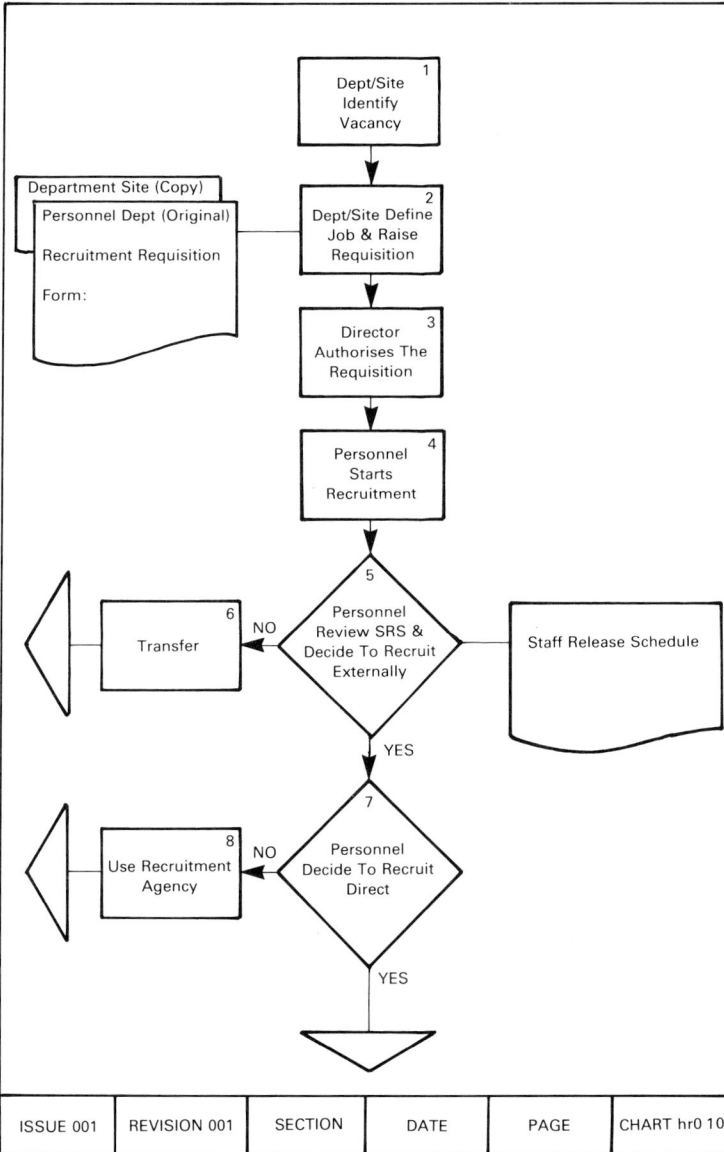

Reproduced with the permission of HR-BC Ltd

Standards Lead Body in their report *A Perspective on Person-nel* published in 1993. The report states:

> The Key Purpose of Personnel is to: enable management
> to enhance the individual and collective contributions of
> people to the short- and long-term success of the enter-
> prise

Note the focus is on Personnel as an enabling function with management as its primary client. This requires responsiveness to both business and operational management needs. As an enabling function, the report says:

> Personnel is concerned with creating an environment
> which enables management to recruit, train and motivate
> the people they need for today's and tomorrow's jobs.

Culture is important. To make change happen, people need to be committed. They need to see that management is commit-ted and that goals and results will be taken seriously. Further-more, staff must be given the opportunity to take on the challenge and the responsibility for making it happen. This principle applies equally within the personnel function. Senior personnel staff need to show commitment with demonstrable hands-on participation. Goals must have tangible targets and resources (time, money and people) need to be allocated to make the initiatives work.

To be enablers or facilitators, the function has to be respected; it must be a source of advice or expertise. This means that skills must be continually enhanced so personnel staff develop in tandem with business needs. Our experience has been that the function sometimes expends all its energy trying to develop everybody else and forgets its own team's needs. The ICL case study (see Chapter 5) provides a wonder-ful example of departmental commitment to excellence and growth.

In my view, to apply the basic quality principles to Personnel demands that the department:

- Identifies and understands what the organisation and line managers expect from Personnel;
- Plans its activities and resources to ensure that these demands are met;
- Ensures monitoring systems are in place to measure the effectiveness of the activities and the response of Personnel's clients;
- Makes sure regular reviews (quarterly or monthly) of procedure and policy provide a basis for constant improvement of services;
- Ascertains that all documents issued by Personnel have both a version and date control to ensure staff using handbooks, forms, policy statements or charts are working with the most up-to-date, relevant release;
- Ensures information systems – both computerised and manual – contain relevant, accurate and timely data. Where this is not the case, the records need to be amended or destroyed.
- Makes certain that a clear training programme is evident *for* the personnel department, to ensure that these processes and procedures can be sustained.

Taking it a stage further

What if the department wishes to take it further, to seek accreditation under a quality standard in its own right? A number of personnel functions have sought to do this (Edmund Nuttall, see Chapter 9, is an example). Others may have been committed to do so as part of corporate TQM initiatives (e.g. Bosch, ICL, etc.).

BS 5750 for the personnel function has little commercial value and is unlikely to be pursued unless the organisation is already pursuing the standard for its core production or service activity. In this respect the personnel function is probably trying to keep pace with other sections or may be trying to set an example for others to follow. The value of the standard, therefore, is the discipline it demands, the need for monitoring and the satisfaction of achieving external recognition (and hence internal respect).

BS 5750/ISO 9000 is a capability standard, i.e. personnel practice meets its declared aims and can be shown to do so through a recognised method of assessment. It is obtained after being assessed by an outside third party of recognised assessors. But it also requires regular inspection by the same group thereafter. It is, therefore, a long-term commitment and must be durable.

What is the standard?

This book does not aim to detail either the BS 5750 standard or how this must be applied to the personnel function. But at this point it is probably worth providing an overview in lay terms.

The British standard for quality systems is known as BS 5750 (sometimes called 'five-seven-five-o', sometimes 'fifty-seven fifty'). It is one of the many standards defined by the British Standards Institution (BSI). Many of these standards were established first for the engineering industry, in particular for those firms supplying military or Government contracts. Over time, the need for such a standard to cover the way products were made was extended to other industries. BS 5750 was drafted in 1979. The standard was then widened in scope in 1987 so as to have universal application. This was to cover service organisations as well as manufacturers.

Similar moves were taking place in many countries, including the United States, and finally agreement was reached on an international standard known as the ISO 9000 series. There is also a European equivalent (ENO series). For quality systems there is no difference between these three equivalents.

BS 5750/ISO 9000 has a number of parts (some of these only refer to guidance documents), and organisations or personnel departments need to decide which part(s) of the standard they wish to be assessed against. Parts 1, 2 or 3 are the key sections under which organisations usually seek assessment:

- *Part 1* covers the design, development, production, installation and servicing of products.
- *Part 2* covers quality systems geared to producing to 'customer' specifications.
- *Part 3* covers final inspection and testing.

Advice needs to be sought as to exactly which part should be registered for. In the main, Personnel is likely to be covered by Part 2 although development of training courses and materials, for example, would come under Part 1. Assuming this, the following list gives an outline of the areas which need to be defined under Part 2 and then examined.

	Relevant section of BS 5750 Part 2
Management responsibility	4.1
Quality system	4.2
Contract review	4.3
Document control	4.4
Purchasing	4.5
Purchaser supplied products	4.6
Product identification and traceability	4.7
Process control	4.8
Inspection and testing	4.9
Inspection measuring and test equipment	4.10
Inspection test status	4.11
Control of non-conforming products	4.12
Corrective action	4.13
Handling, storage, packaging and delivery	4.14
Quality records	4.15
Internal quality audits	4.16
Training	4.17
Statistical techniques	4.18

Some of the terminology used seems hard to apply to person-

nel activity but once you have got to grips with the requirements of each section, it becomes relatively easy to see the
relevance of the sections to the work of the department.

You should carefully plan how to implement such a programme and note that its scope will be wider than the
department itself: by definition it will be a quality assessment
of human resource management across the company.

There are nine broad stages to achieve certification (see page
67).

Documenting quality practice

For most departments this is the most difficult and demanding
stage. Key activities must be documented to be able to
demonstrate intention and control. It requires at least three
separate levels of documentation as shown in Figure 4.4.

Departmental quality manual

This needs to define the objectives, strategies and quality
policy of the department. It need not be lengthy but it must
include a description about how the quality framework is
organised.

The quality manual is the prime reference document outlining the scope of the quality system, the distribution method,
change control, the quality policy, the system objectives and
management responsibility for the quality system. The management representative must have sufficient seniority and
authority to ensure that quality issues are identified and
actioned.

Written procedures and instructions

Under given activity headings, a set of procedures covering all
activities undertaken by staff within the department needs to

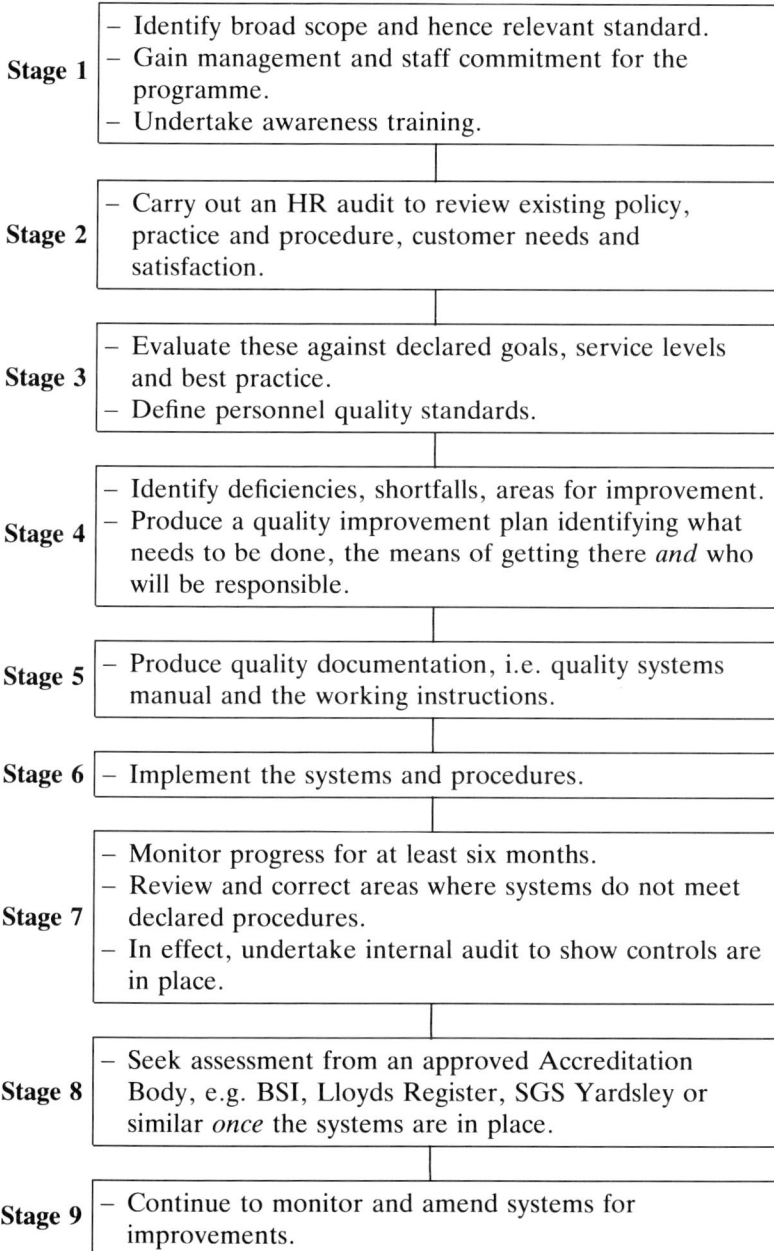

Stage 1	– Identify broad scope and hence relevant standard. – Gain management and staff commitment for the programme. – Undertake awareness training.
Stage 2	– Carry out an HR audit to review existing policy, practice and procedure, customer needs and satisfaction.
Stage 3	– Evaluate these against declared goals, service levels and best practice. – Define personnel quality standards.
Stage 4	– Identify deficiencies, shortfalls, areas for improvement. – Produce a quality improvement plan identifying what needs to be done, the means of getting there *and* who will be responsible.
Stage 5	– Produce quality documentation, i.e. quality systems manual and the working instructions.
Stage 6	– Implement the systems and procedures.
Stage 7	– Monitor progress for at least six months. – Review and correct areas where systems do not meet declared procedures. – In effect, undertake internal audit to show controls are in place.
Stage 8	– Seek assessment from an approved Accreditation Body, e.g. BSI, Lloyds Register, SGS Yardsley or similar *once* the systems are in place.
Stage 9	– Continue to monitor and amend systems for improvements.

Figure 4.4
Documenting quality practice

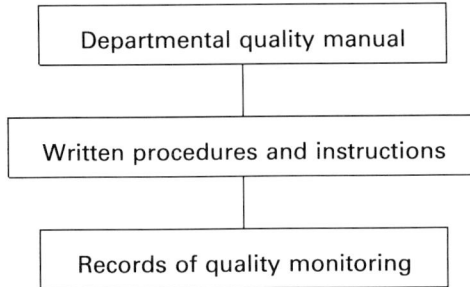

```
┌─────────────────────────────────────────┐
│     Departmental quality manual          │
└─────────────────────────────────────────┘
                     │
┌─────────────────────────────────────────┐
│  Written procedures and instructions     │
└─────────────────────────────────────────┘
                     │
┌─────────────────────────────────────────┐
│     Records of quality monitoring        │
└─────────────────────────────────────────┘
```

be documented. Clearly it is important that this describes the purpose and scope of each activity and accurately describes how it should be carried out. It needs to identify who is responsible for each procedure and must show how it is linked to the overall framework.

Each identified procedure needs to be signed off by the quality representative for approval.

Day-to-day working practice. This section must illustrate the order and sequence of activities and hence will comprise any forms, charts or records used.

Records of quality monitoring

Quality records. The system must also ensure that records of internal audits, non-conformance and corrective actions are available to give evidence that the system is being monitored. Audits, both internal and external, need to be carried out against a planned programme and by individuals independent of the various activities.

Format. The key to success is to ensure that all documents are written in a simple, fixed format. Each document must be clearly identifiable through the following:

- Procedure number
- Issue status (date or version number)
- Page numbering
- Approval signature.

The area where most systems initially fail is that of document control – either in terms of identifying the current version or in terms of ensuring the removal and destruction of earlier, outdated versions.

Time frame

As illustrated in the brief overview above, a lot of work needs to be undertaken to meet a quality standard, whether this is BS 5750/ISO 9000 or a company TQM requirement. The time should not be underestimated. For most personnel departments, it is likely to take anything between nine and eighteen months. The charts in Figures 4.5 and 4.6 show the timetables established by one organisation for the implementation of its audit programme.

If you are starting now you can benefit to some extent from the experience of others, but detailed analysis and documentation of *your* personnel policy and practice will still be required.

The timelag inevitably means some initiatives run the risk of running out of steam. If members of the team are not allocated sufficient time and assistance, it is likely that the improvement programme will fail. The programme must therefore be given project status and a clear priority. It should also be considered a departmental project not simply a responsibility for individuals to complete and document their own areas of activity. As a team activity it can provide an often needed unity, allowing personnel administrators to work more closely to the management group.

But the team also need a number of 'quick wins' so that progress is visible and celebrated. Improving the quality of HR

Figure 4.5
HR Quality programme schedule

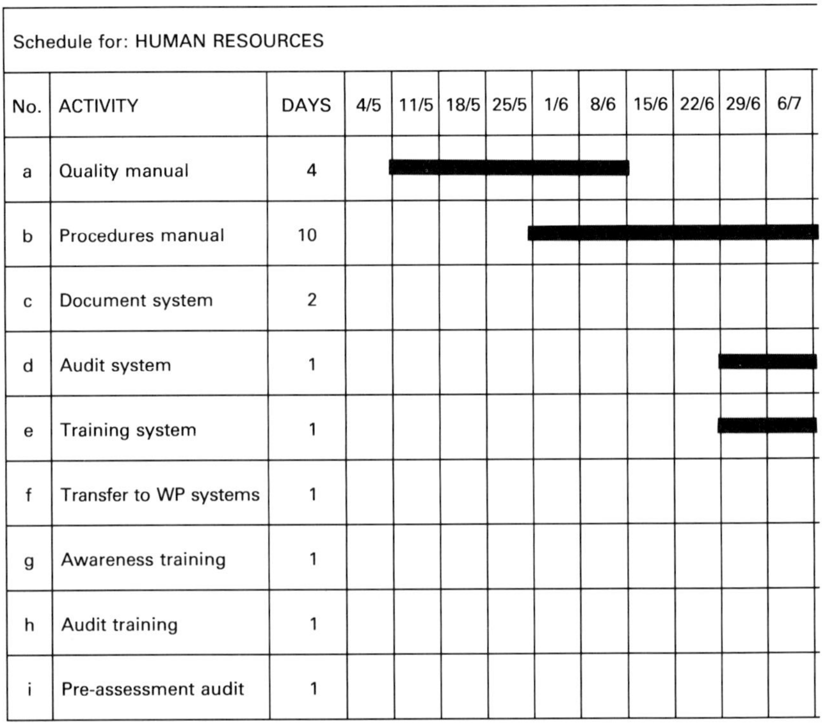

Schedule for: HUMAN RESOURCES

No.	ACTIVITY	DAYS	4/5	11/5	18/5	25/5	1/6	8/6	15/6	22/6	29/6	6/7
a	Quality manual	4		▬▬▬▬▬▬								
b	Procedures manual	10				▬▬▬▬▬▬▬▬						
c	Document system	2										
d	Audit system	1									▬▬	
e	Training system	1									▬▬	
f	Transfer to WP systems	1										
g	Awareness training	1										
h	Audit training	1										
i	Pre-assessment audit	1										

Reproduced with the permission of Edmund Nuttal Ltd

reports (as demonstrated in the Glaxo and KLM case studies, Chapters 7 and 6 respectively) or giving line managers flow-charts and effective personnel forms (as illustrated in the Edmund Nuttall case study, Chapter 9) are good examples of high-profile wins.

We would like to, but . . .

For some departments, particularly in medium or smaller-sized organisations, such plans may seem totally unrealistic. If you

															Date: 01.05.92	
13/7	20/7	27/7	3/8	10/8	17/8	24/8	31/8	7/9	14/9	21/9	28/9	5/10	12/10	19/10	26/10	2/11

are already under intense pressure on workloads, it is often hard to make the space to plan such a programme let alone consider implementing it. But we all need to improve our contribution.

Another way of improving effectiveness and the quality of HR practice is to pilot a particular area – but choose one with wide exposure. Improving absence control or recruitment administration would be suitable examples. In this way the department can make improvements, test techniques and gain confidence without overloading resources in an all-out campaign.

Adopting quality assessment will lead to greater efficiencies,

Figure 4.6
Internal audit plan – HR function

Section	Auditor	1993								
		Jan	Feb	Mar	Apr	May	Jun	Jul	Aug	Sep
Personnel										
• Recruitment	R J D	★								
• Pay & benefits	G D M									★
Pensions										
• Pensions	G D M				★					
• Medical	R J D			★						
• Insurance	G D M									
Training										
• Course administration	B F M	★								
• CITB	B F M							★		
• Training	B F M						★			
• HR Training	G D H									★
Systems										
• Computer administration	R J D					★				
Quality										
• Quality system administration	R J D		★						★	
H.R. Management										
• Organisation effectiveness	H L H									
• Business objectives	H L H									

and thus savings in time, if three fundamental concepts are put into practice:

- Simplify and clarify
- Seek and define the purpose
- Deliver what the organisation and line managers require, not what the department thinks they need.

Case Studies

5

▨ Maximising the Department's Potential – ICL

This case study illustrates how ICL, and ICL Europe in particular, has reviewed the personnel function, aligned it to business needs and, importantly, has established quality standards and best practice within the function. ICL has placed great emphasis on people development and the personnel function is no exception. With 150 personnel professionals serving some 24,000 employees in Europe, the HR function is key but it is also under continuous change with a need to demonstrate its ability to add value to the organisation. ICL is one of largest companies to achieve the Investors in People (IIP) award.

Corporate background

ICL is now a major success story – it has been one of the few profitable companies in the information technology sector for the past three years. But it was not always so. In the early 1980s ICL was in serious financial trouble but, with STC ownership in 1984 and the subsequent sale of the major shareholding to Fujitsu in 1990, the organisation is now part of the second largest IT company in the world.

A new management team, a new culture based on customer-oriented Total Quality Management plus focused markets in Europe have brought success and a reputation for excellence. It has been a remarkable turn-round, particularly during a time of deepening recession and intense competition.

The success can be largely attributed to three guiding principles:

• *Investment in people.* The Chairman's Statement in the ICL

PLC Corporate Review 1992 starts with the heading: 'Success is led by people first and product second'. The report states:

> Putting sophisticated technology to work for customers requires the active participation of a creative team. That is why our contribution to our customers' success depends first and foremost on the calibre of our people. It is why we spend heavily – £20m in 1992 – on staff training and the systematic development of our employees' potential.

- *Flexibility and adaptability*. ICL was the first of the major computer manufacturers to 're-engineer' its business. It moved from low-volume, high-margin, predominately mainframe hardware sales, to higher-volume business based on a combination of software, hardware and service delivery. One analyst has said 'ICL has the open systems business right, the PC business right, the third-party channel right, and it appears to be getting the services business right too'. While other major computer manufacturers, notably IBM and Wang, have suffered record losses, ICL is one of the few still reporting profits.

  To be responsive to customers demands flexibility and adaptability. Project teams need to be able to select and call on appropriate resources to match customer expectations. The company must be forward looking. ICL has to ensure that the skills of its employees are constantly upgraded to meet the challenges of tomorrow. In addition, the organisation itself needs to be lean, nimble and responsive to the market.

  This required a change in culture. Decision-making has been devolved to line managers, risk and entrepreneurial activity is encouraged and a major empowerment exercise is underway. This has meant traditional procedures and systems have been reassessed and in many cases removed. This sea change has had major implications for personnel.

- *Quality*. ICL was one of the first UK organisations to embrace Total Quality Management (TQM). This affects every level of the business and everybody in the business. It is not just a pursuit for BS 5750 or ISO 9000 certification. It is a corporate goal and value in its own right.

Once again this is best illustrated from the Chairman's Statement in the Corporate Review:

> Our goal is to exceed our customers' expectations and to delight them with personal service; we call it Customer Care. Conformance to requirements, the usual definition of quality is no longer enough. Our computers are expected to be reliable and our service organisation is geared to respond efficiently. If Customer Care is one critical success factor, the other is continuous improvement . . . we have introduced a continuous improvement process called Delta, the aim of which is to 'improve a thousand things by 1 per cent rather than one thing by 1000 per cent'.

The impact of change

As described, for ICL the last decade has seen turbulent and massive cultural change. What has been the impact on the personnel function of these changes in the business and the organisation structure?

1 *Sold as a major investment to a Japanese company*

As a result of separation from the previous parent (STC plc) the immediate impact was on a number of benefit entitlements – notably a restructuring of the pension scheme and share option arrangement. But it also demanded a reassessment and adjustment of strategy plus a wider 'international outlook'.

2 *Acquisition and merger of other companies*

Part of ICL's growth has been the acquisition and merger of several other organisations, including manufacturing and development facilities. Personnel, in many respects, needed to manage such mergers and ensure smooth integration – with all its ramifications – on shifting resources, communication of culture, alignment and implementation of strategy, review and adoption of personnel policy.

3 *New markets, new freedoms*

The opening up of new business markets and the encouragement of entrepreneurial activity also required Personnel to give up many of the trappings of control (notably personnel and pay policies which restricted activity). Retraining was necessary, plus reassessment of overheads.

4 *Recession*

The IT industry has been in marked recession, especially after its massive expansion in the 1960s and 70s. Large numbers of jobs have been shed and many people moved to new roles demanding counselling and retraining respectively.

5 *Electronic communications*

ICL has also been at the forefront of utilising electronic and video communication within the organisation. There is a new worldwide electronic mailing system so everyone has a VDU terminal and screen on their desk. Video conferencing and distance learning have been introduced. The HR impact is that information and communication is now instantly accessible and expectation for such information is high. It also means that staff can work from a number of locations, whether this is an office or home, and patterns of work have altered. The roles of secretaries and managers have changed considerably, with the former more obviously support administrators rather than typists, and the latter becoming far more computer-literate, undertaking hands-on report writing and modelling.

Within this context Personnel has to ensure that HR data is available and accurate. Personnel needs to respond more quickly and strategically. Speed of access in terms of information and communication has had a direct impact on the need for more analysis and interpretation.

The process of change

The process of change is dynamic and ICL is one the few organisations that recognises that the turbulence of the past decade will not cease. Instead it has seen this turbulence as an opportunity. Consequently the role of HR will not get easier; there will be new challenges which the function needs to anticipate and prepare for.

ICL has made several large and small acquisitions and established a number of joint ventures. Personnel is intimately involved in the subsequent integration process. The function notes the failure rate of many mergers in terms of realising their initial objectives. Too often the HR function is left with the implementation and integration of a business plan that was over-optimistic and underrated HR issues. The experience of the past 10 years within ICL Europe has taught Personnel to recognise that it is to cultural changes, loss of identity and loss of skills which more often than not cause failure. The function is therefore seeking to minimise these issues by anticipating the problems in advance.

Second, the almost constant requirement to restructure due to changing margins has meant that managerial levels need to be reduced, and decision-making and accountability accelerated and pushed downwards. Personnel needs to help facilitate these flatter structures and assist empowerment. Career development is also likely to change from hierarchical promotions to greater skill and responsibility attainment.

Third, although ICL has always been internationally minded, it focused predominantly on the European market. It now sees that there is pressure for globalisation and that this demands strategies which require international thinking on every front.

Fourth, competition will intensify. There is constant pressure to reduce costs, improve productivity and increase speed of delivery. But this needs to be matched against rising levels of customer demands for quality and service. The impact is that all activities are now carefully monitored.

Fifth, IT and telecommunications will continue to advance at a staggering pace. This will also see increasing use of shared or networked database information through the use of 'open systems'.

Responding to the challenges

The need to respond to these trends will have an impact on wider human resource management for the company in four main areas:

- *Organisation and culture*. Team working must increase but this also requires better leaders of teams. The need for corporate processes, procedures and reporting levels will reduce. In the main, operations will be simplified. Spans of control are likely to increase partly through fewer levels of management, and partly through multiple and cross-functional reporting. Most significantly ICL has started to question exactly what empowerment means. Each line manager has been asked to benchmark their roles against best practice both within and outside the organisation. Table 5.1 summarises some of the questions that managers have been asked to consider.
- *Pay and benefits*. A more flexible organisation also demands flexible people. This means jobs should not be constrained by set descriptions or grades which potentially

Table 5.1
The reality of empowerment

The test of empowerment strategies can be identified through the
following questions:

- Do we have minimum managerial levels?
- Do we have maximum practical delegation of authority?
- Do we have simple approval processes?
- Do we have person-to-person communication, not by memo?
- Do we have minimum rules, procedures and reporting
  requirements?
- Have we eliminated non-productive activities?
- Do we liberate the talent of individuals to take initiatives for
  themselves?
- Do we place decisions closest to the point of impact?
- Do all people feel a sense of owning the enterprise?
- Is everybody undertaking competitive benchmarking?
- Do we have responsive, co-operative structures with teams
  working for the common good?

limit actions. Traditional job evaluation is now being
reviewed with a new broader role banding, and the focus of
pay and benefits is moving from paying for a *job* to paying
people for their performance, competence and experience.
Pay is also determined by budgets rather than some
national scale. More flexibility is being introduced to allow
managers to consider and plan pay in their area within a set
budget.

- *Resourcing.* Increased mobility of staff, especially within
  the EC, has led the personnel function to be 'European' in
  outlook. ICL actively encourages the mobility of younger
  people through a 'Eurograduate' scheme while also targeting wider recruitment and selection. For example, ICL in
  the UK looks to recruit 10 per cent of its graduate intake
  from Continental Europe.

The Eurograduate scheme trains young people from
different countries together, ensuring a wider appreciation
of the European business requirements. After a short
period of two months in their home country, Euro-
graduates spend a further 10 months on work experience

projects in UK-based offices, and attend common courses including product awareness and language skill development.

The personnel function is also strongly involved with alternative work patterns – for example, homeworking, teleworking, and variable contracts – some of which ICL is acknowledged as having pioneered for the past few years.

- *People development.* While the number of hierarchical promotions may reduce, ICL still needs to manage employee development and individual careers. The difference is that the emphasis is now on skill, capability and experience rather than managerial responsibility. Furthermore, individual development is likely to require a broader skill base. More care is also required in defining roles, as the reduced number of promotional steps will inevitably mean employees requiring higher job satisfaction since individuals will be spending longer periods in each role.

The impact on Personnel

The role of the human resource professional within ICL is changing. Under the new, flexible organisation much of personnel procedure and practice is being passed down to line managers (or being scrapped). There is less administration and less policing.

HR must be seen to add value and, consequently, its role must be more strategic and forward-looking. ICL (UK) has undertaken a major review of the personnel function to give a model of how it should develop in the light of the changing business requirements.

Not only does the new role demand an evolutionary change, but Personnel must also respond at what has been described a 'revolutionary speed'. With Professor David Guest of Birbeck College and senior representatives of the UK personnel team, interviews were held with members of the ICL board of

Table 5.2
Shifts in style and focus

From	To
Short-term, reactive, marginal activity	Longer-term, proactive, strategic, integrated activity
Controlling	Devolving to line managers
Collective, low trust group policies	An environment of greater trust to individual managers
Mechanistic systems with high administration	Flexible, less bureaucratic guidelines
Professional specialists	Business team integration
Compliance	Commitment
Cost minimisation	Resource effectiveness

directors and senior managers. A second phase of interviews was conducted with a wider sample of middle and junior managers. The key results showed a need to shift style and focus in certain major areas (see Table 5.2).

One of the accusations has been that Personnel was viewed as bureaucratic. This was analysed as follows:

- A lack of trust, expressed through excessive authorisation levels
- Undue requests for information
- Excessive supply of information
- Over-engineered processes which masquerade as professionalism, cause excessive paperwork and substitute for managerial judgement
- Confused accountabilities
- Cumbersome decision-making processes
- A preference for paper-to-people rather than people-to-people communication.

In essence line managers wanted greater day-to-day responsibility for decisions but did not want to take on board the administrative tasks devolved. The personnel team equally recognise the need to improve administrative systems, otherwise the function may find itself excluded from important decision-making forums, irrespective of individual capabilities. In essence, the personnel function had to manage significant change in its own role.

Personnel in transition

In the light of the challenges the personnel team agreed that the overriding objectives and purposes of the function were:

- Personnel exists to support the achievement of business goals.
- This is achieved by translating business plans into integrated human resource plans.
- ICL is committed to valuing its employees and the notion of teamwork.
- Personnel needs to be creative and assertive in the management of change.

In addition, the function must ensure that the organisation operates in a legal, decent and honest way.

Furthermore the group identified five distinct roles within the function as follows:

- *Company-wide expert*. Leading-edge expert on specialist subject(s) available to whole organisation.
- *Experienced specialist adviser/helper*. Sufficient expertise in an area of HR to provide routine guidance and assistance. May be a full- or part-time role.
- *Business team specialist*. Fully contributes to business team in HRM through benchmarking, depth of experience and personal credibility. The individual is capable of operating in strategic roles.
- *Developing generalist*. Provides a general personnel service to the business team in terms of efficient personnel process and day-to-day problem solving.

- *Administrator server.* Maintains efficient personnel procedures and systems.

As the organisation develops, these roles may need revision. But for each of them, the function has identified the requirements in terms of knowledge, skills, attitudes and experience (ICL's version of competencies). All personnel staff are placed into one of the roles in relation to the role currently performed plus the role to which they are aspiring. This helps identify skills required now and for the future.

ICL is firmly committed to skill development in terms of both self-development for the individual and the obligations of the manager. This is supported by ICL's 'Investing in People' programme which provides an integrated approach to combining people development systems, including performance management, appraisal and development.

In addition, ICL has a process of business review every four months. Part of the review considers organisation and people development, where line managers are required to present to fellow managers issues affecting organisation structure, skill requirements and training needs. It also focuses on key individuals and those individuals with high potential.

The personnel function carries out similar reviews for its professional staff every six months so that a development plan assesses each member of the team in terms of roles, potential, need for moves and resourcing requirements.

Special programmes for the personnel function

The personnel team has developed a series of specialised seminars for personnel professionals. These vary in length from two to four days and are typically run two or three times each year. The topics include:

- Understanding the Business
- The Personnel Function and its Role

- Employment
- Health and Safety
- Remuneration
- Resourcing
- People Development
- Training and Development
- Organisation Design.

Each module is owned and hosted by one of the senior line personnel directors. The brief not only covers a basic grounding in the topic but specifically explores new ideas, directions and skills needed for the future.

In addition there are specialised skill courses in:

- Counselling
- Developing Individual Capability
- Skill-based Interviewing
- Training the Trainer, etc.

Setting the standards

The previous sections have outlined the function's commitment to reassessing its role in the light of business requirements and the need to present innovative, forward-looking, proactive policies. Even these intentions may not deliver credibility.

The function has therefore defined standards of personnel performance for the ideal personnel/HR function, including both hard and soft measures of performance. As described earlier, this represents a standard to aim for – a personal, departmental and corporate benchmark for the HR professional. Such standards will require review as the business demands; they cannot be set in concrete. ICL's HR standards are reproduced opposite.

ICL PLC – Human Resource Standards

1   General
1.1   The senior Personnel Manager/VP is an effective member of the Unit's business team, understands and can discuss competently the key business issues, and contributes to the business decisions.
1.2   All personnel practices and procedures comply with the letter and spirit of the law, and maintain and promote the highest standards of integrity.
1.3   All personnel practices and procedures do not discriminate unfairly on the basis of age, sex, religion, race, nationality, marital or handicap status.
1.4   All personnel practices, procedures and programmes are consistent with the values of the ICL Way, and are positively promoted through induction and other programmes, together with other cultural norms/processes agreed as important for ICL.
1.5   The ICL Quality Process is operated fully in the personnel function, and sets of requirements are used as the basis of measurement.
1.6   All members of the function have been trained in the quality process, and are measuring conformance in an agreed way.
1.7   Wherever feasible, encouragement is given to young personnel trainees or students to provide projects/experience etc.
1.8   Standards are laid down for the professionalism and business knowledge of each staff member in Personnel, and training given as needed.
1.9   The personnel function is seen as an example in practice of the processes it seeks to promote.
1.10   Monthly reports are submitted to HQ by the 6th of each month, and local reporting requirements are fully met.
1.11   Standards of environment and housekeeping in offices of the function are beyond criticism.
1.12   An up-to-date manual is maintained summarising corporate and local policies/procedures, and distribution to managers is controlled.

2   Resourcing and Recruitment
2.1   A manpower plan looking four quarters ahead is produced each quarter.
2.2   A longer-term strategic resourcing plan, identifying skill shifts and key resourcing/re-profiling/training requirements, is an integral part of the strategy plan for the business.
2.3   A plan for recruiting and training young entrants is made every year as part of the plans above.

2.4   Key resource ratios (% sales, % service, % other) are agreed annually in support of the business plan and specified.

2.5   The balance of permanent to non-permanent resource is part of the manpower plan in 2.1, and derived from the local OPEX budgets and business plans.

2.6   In recognition of the role in image marketing that recruitment plays, there are:
        (i)   company promotional literature.
        (ii)   statements of requirements specified for recruitment timescales, particularly in dealing with prospective candidates, and measurement maintained against these.
        (iii)   standards for speedy and friendly dealing with speculative enquiries.
        (iv)   standards of advertising consistent with an ICL quality image and local image-building strategies.
        (v)   promotion of IT industry and ICL as appropriate with young people.

2.7   Methods are available for notifying vacancies/opportunities to current staff prior to commissioning external recruitment.

2.8   Rolling three-month attrition rates are calculated and analysed monthly.

2.9   Selection methods are more broadly based than use of an interview alone, and utilise best internal or external practice.

2.10   All management involved in recruiting have had specialised training in recruitment and selection.

2.11   All personnel staff involved in recruiting have had specialised training in recruitment and selection, including occupational testing as appropriate.

2.12   A personnel professional trained in recruitment is involved in every selection process.

2.13   Person specifications and job descriptions exist for each recruitment task.

2.14   All offer letters and contracts are controlled by Personnel.

2.15   All new employees receive company, division, departmental and personal induction training.

2.16   All voluntary leavers have exit interviews which are documented.

2.17   Company and legal standards on the use and administration of psychological tests or assessment materials are compiled with.

3   Training and Development

3.1   OMRs covering the full spectrum of organisational and individual development issues are held in each business at least every six months.

3.2   An appraisal system is in place which conforms to ICL group standards, which reviews performance against agreed objectives, develops action plans for performance improvement and defines plans for training and development.

3.3   All managers have been trained in giving face-to-face constructive appraisals.

3.4   Appraisals are conducted with each employee at least annually.

3.5   Each employee has a job description and a clear definition of his/her standards of performance and/or period objectives.

3.6   A training plan exists based on the needs of the business and on a summary of individual training requirements, and specific supporting budgets are in place.

3.7   Employees with significant shortfalls on personal performance are being placed on a plan for improvement, with objectives and dates, with clear consequences understood for failure at each step.

3.8   Performance ratings are given to each employee which summarise performance against objectives, according to the company definition.

3.19   Each employee is assessed at least annually on his or her potential for promotion to greater responsibility, based on the company classification of potential.

3.10   For each employee with 'upwards' potential, career development plans are in place based on reaching the next 'career aiming point'.

3.11   Succession plans for the top two levels of management are an integral part of the OMR.

3.12   A positive approach to putting forward individuals for international assignments, and to receiving them for development, is a reality; individuals are identified each year through appraisals.

3.13   Each business has identified positions in the organisation that are suitable for a non-national to fill.

3.14   Each business has a programme, and/or local processes, for providing added value development for individuals (junior boards, projects, etc.) with potential.

3.15   A re-profiling plan, name by name, is prepared each year for appropriate groups of employees.

3.16   The nomination of individuals for courses is based on an identified need, and a reminder is given to all delegates' managers of the need to follow up with the delegate the lessons of the course.

3.17   All qualifying managers have been nominated for the appropriate 'core' level course.

3.18   Where appropriate, facilities are provided for language training and employees positively encouraged to use them.

3.19   Career structures are agreed and published for all major streams.

3.20   CVs exist for all management and high potential staff that include the current position.

4   Organisation Development

4.1   The organisation structure is designed to support company and local strategies and give necessary focus.

4.2   Departments have a clear statement of accountabilities for results which do not overlap.

4.3   Where matrix structures exist, the network of functional relationships is understood and accountabilities are clear.

4.4   Opinion surveys (or other cultural instruments) are conducted and analysed, and lead to an action plan at least once a year in each area.

4.5   Organisation change is professionally managed, with a documented communication plan, full statements outlining the change, and questions/answers where appropriate.

4.6   Organisation charts are always available and are updated quarterly.

4.7   Team building events are used as appropriate to provide commitment to common goals.

5   Remuneration and Benefits

5.1   Targets for paycost and compensation/revenue are set each year and managed.

5.2   All jobs are defined and evaluated using an ICL-approved system, and employees are made aware of grades for their jobs.

5.3   As much as possible of the pay increase programme is related to performance in the job, encapsulated in a performance rating that is communicated fully to each individual employee.

5.4   The distribution of increases against performance is significant.

5.5   A market position has been agreed with management as a standard, and surveys are carried out with competitors and consultant bodies over a meaningful range of jobs to establish that position.

5.6   The approach to pay and benefits is communicated to and understood by all employees.

5.7   All legal reporting requirements are fully observed, and all systems of payment conform to the law.

5.8   Bonus schemes in use are approved by ICL and promote reward for individual or team effort over and above their 'normal job'.

5.9   Pay plans are produced on time and in the format required by the guidelines issued annually.

5.10   Benefits systems are the same for all employees, unless hierarchical discrimination is dictated by the market or by tax effectiveness.

5.11   Legal tax-efficient forms of remuneration and benefits are exploited consistent with competitive market practice.

5.12   Salary and benefit scales/regulations are complied with by all managers, and appropriate authority levels for approval of change are used for control.

5.13   Bonus scheme targets based on a company year are all issued before the end of January.

5.14   Dates for pay reviews/approvals are always complied with.

6   Employee Relations

6.1   A strategy and action plan for employee communication is determined and reviewed annually.

6.2   All employees are aware of grievance and disciplinary procedures which are written up and available.

6.3   Legal requirements for employee representation are complied with but nevertheless an ongoing programme of action exists where necessary to minimise the need for and the involvement of third parties.

6.4   Opinion surveys show that at least 75% of the population are knowledgeable of company and local goals.

7   Administration and Systems

7.1   Personnel records are complete, up to date and automated.

7.2   Personnel departments are a 'Productivity Showcase', using latest technology, and can be used for customer demonstrations if necessary.

7.3   Confidentiality of all personal information is maintained and relevant legislation on data protection complied with. All manual and automated information systems are secure.

7.4   Staff have access to information held on their personal files or databases unless specific exceptions have been notified to them. These exceptions will be information which is confidential to a third party.

7.5   A budget is included annually for the development of improved systems and department productivity.

7.6   Local policies and procedures are clearly written up, are up to date and available as needed.

7.7   Local requirements are specified for the administration procedures; and performance measured against them annually.

7.8   A rating on a scale 1–10 of Personal service from line management is regularly > 8.

Conclusion

Personnel within ICL is under pressure to deliver more for less but at the same time to add more value to the organisation in order to justify its existence. To achieve this the function has changed radically: it has reviewed its role and its perceptions in the light of the business requirements; it has taken note of criticisms and improved its service by assessing the current HR skill base and the needs for the future; it has set up a development programme *for* the function and has published a set of standards as goals.

6

Innovative IT in Personnel – KLM Royal Dutch Airlines

KLM's UK personnel department has an extremely high level of administrative effectiveness in terms of response to requests for information from management, employees and applicants alike. This has been achieved through the use of information technology within the department. By linking 12 PC-based software packages, the use of IT covers all aspects: recruitment and selection; personnel records; training; time and attendance; payroll; word processing; and pension administration.

One of the key elements in this success story is that all members of the department are involved and have responsibility for specific applications. It also represents one of the few examples where cost savings from the introduction of computer systems has not only been calculated but shown to be significant. The department's achievement was recognised by winning the national IPM/Percom award for Innovation in Technology in Personnel (ITIP) in 1991.

Background

KLM Royal Dutch Airlines was one of the first passenger airlines. Its tradition has always been based on quality of service. The airline flies to over 159 cities in 83 countries around the world and employs over 25,500 employees. In addition to its 8 million passenger service, it carries 849 million tonnes of cargo.

In recent years the increasing competitiveness of the airline business has led KLM to form partnerships with a number of other airlines in terms of joint operations.

In the UK and Ireland, KLM employs 650 staff at some 12 locations from Aberdeen in the North of Scotland to the

Channel Islands. The main location is Heathrow Airport in London. The staff include baggage handlers, ticket reservation, marketing and sales personnel plus a head office support function.

Use of IT within airlines

The airline industry has always been at the forefront of information technology. In 1949 the industry set up a co-operative society to provide worldwide telecommunication services which now serves over 300 airlines in 170 countries. These are used to handle airline central reservations which amount to over 10 billion messages a year – all in real-time.

Direct communication links exist between KLM in Holland and the UK and, within the UK operations, smaller local area networks (LANs) have been established.

Consequently there is an expectation that information is accurate and is available instantly from all parts of the organisation. Not surprisingly this sets quite a target for personnel operations.

Role of Personnel

Personnel departments receive and collate vast amounts of information – not all are totally successful in processing and distributing it. For the KLM UK personnel function, accessability and speed of response are prime criteria for judging their effectiveness.

The department consists of five people, each with a defined area of responsibility as shown in Figure 6.1.

Setting priorities

In 1986 the department recognised that it needed to reorganise and improve the service provided. This was partly to meet

Figure 6.1
Organisation chart for KLM's UK personnel function

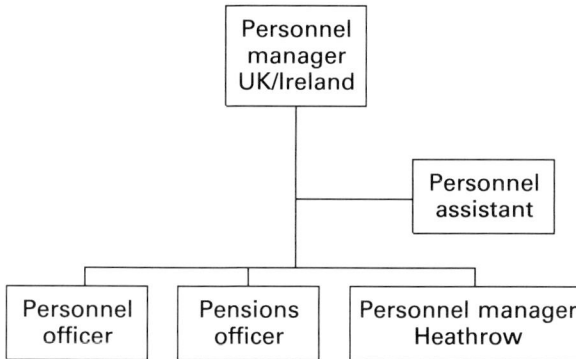

```
            ┌─────────────┐
            │  Personnel  │
            │   manager   │
            │  UK/Ireland │
            └──────┬──────┘
                   │        ┌──────────────┐
                   ├────────│  Personnel   │
                   │        │  assistant   │
                   │        └──────────────┘
       ┌───────────┼────────────────────┐
┌──────┴─────┐ ┌───┴────┐ ┌─────────────┴──────┐
│ Personnel  │ │Pensions│ │ Personnel manager  │
│  officer   │ │officer │ │     Heathrow       │
└────────────┘ └────────┘ └────────────────────┘
```

ever-increasing workloads (while under pressure to do so
without additional staff); to create an information resource
(i.e. to become proactive in effective use of data); to influence
change within the organisation at a time of rising commercial
pressure; and to change the image and profile of Personnel as
perceived within the company.

The availability of relatively cheap PC-based packages
provided the means to professionalise the department, which
had been frustrated in its long wait for a corporate solution to
be delivered.

Unlike some organisations KLM has sought to use IT for all
elements of personnel operations if possible. As a result, no
one package is seen in isolation. This is important since it
demands that all data is being used for a purpose and the whole
remains an integrated project. For many organisations a
computerised personnel information system (CPIS) is seen as a
record-keeping system and becomes an electronic filing cabi-
net. For KLM, many of its packages are linked, directly or
indirectly, using the transfer of files to reduce duplication of
input and, more importantly, to provide speedy access and
response.

A further feature of KLM's strategy has been the thorough

investigation of available packages in the marketplace. This
demands an appreciation of what to look for plus a requirement that any package chosen must be able to import and
export data to other packages easily without recourse to
computer specialists. Integration in this case, therefore, does
not mean one suite of software from a single supplier.

Internal reorganisation

In 1986 the department decided that a computerised personnel
information system was vital if the function was to provide
information of sufficient quality and at an acceptable speed for
line managers.

In preparation for this project, the personnel manager was
conscious of the need to reorganise the roles of staff within the
department and to ensure each had either the required skills or
the aptitude to acquire them. One member, who was nearing
retirement age, did not wish to change the non-computerised
habits of a lifetime and opted for early retirement.

The members of the department are in the main young,
computer literate and very enthusiastic. All these characteristics were relevant in helping to bring about the change in both
the operation and image of the department.

Selection of packages

Personnel records

Prior to selection and purchase, the department spent three
days identifying the needs and specifications for such a system.
This again is an important, but often neglected, fundamental
requirement. The personnel manager says that this investment
in planning time has paid dividends ever since.

The core of the project was the selection of a personnel

administration system. This met the principal criteria of being easy-to-use, providing sufficient flexibility to add or tailor records and allowing import or export of information to other packages.

It is also a multi-user system, thereby allowing each member access for both input or output across the department's network. Again this is important as it ensures that data can be accessed by everybody within the department and is not the sole responsibility of one individual. Many personnel departments make the mistake of introducing a single-user system which becomes one person's prime task. First, access is limited, knowledge is dangerously concentrated and others in the department cannot get involved. This limits development of the system's use and often results in a major problem should the individual leave or others look to change how the department operates.

Significantly, the personnel manager adds all new starters or salary changes into the system personally. This ensures that he is using the system, and is aware of all new starts, leaves or changes of job, grade or salary. The amount of input takes approximately one hour per day but he says it is well worth it in terms of remaining up-to-date operationally. Unlike many other system implementations that I have been involved in, the personal interest of the head of department means that everybody understands the importance of the system; it retains a 'project status' and is used to help formulate both strategy and policy. It also means that everyone handles requests for information and that senior manager, line manager or employee requests are dealt with immediately – not third hand or by transferring telephone calls.

Flexibility is also important – the department has tailored the package to meet specific KLM requirements, for example:

• Identity card renewals
• Industrial accident records
• Medical and travel insurance information
• Test results

- Training records
- Uniform issue.

But a further and crucial element in selection was the need to interface the personnel system with other software used by the department. This includes the following applications:

- Interviewing
- Candidate testing
- Salary/wage modelling
- Pensions (administration is undertaken in-house)
- Training
- Job evaluation
- Electronic time recording
- Staff rostering
- Payroll
- Organisation charting
- Word processing/desk top publishing.

The plan, or schema, showing how these packages are linked is shown in Figure 6.2.

Allocating responsibility

Five people work within the personnel and pensions department. One of the reasons why the systems are so effective is that each member of the department has been assigned responsibility for one or more of the 12 software packages, their application and development. This concept of data ownership is seen as crucial by the personnel manager. This is illustrated below:

The personnel manager is responsible for keeping the main personnel database up to date. This is a daily hands-on operation (rarely seen elsewhere) but only requires on average one hour per day adding joiners, adjusting salaries, taking out

Figure 6.2

Illustrative chart of personnel systems and their links

KLM Royal Dutch Airlines (UK)
Personnel departmment – Information technology

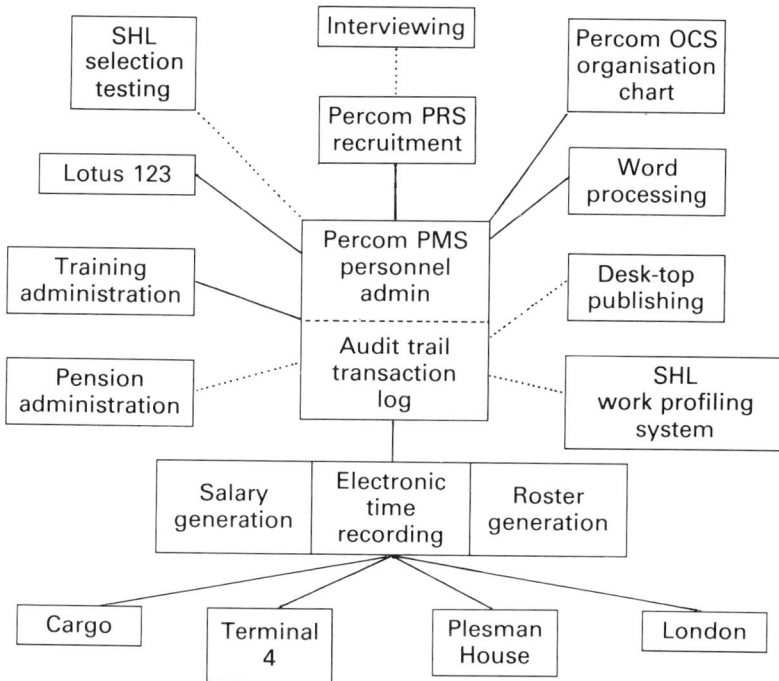

—— Direct link
······ Indirect link

Reproduced with the permission of KLM Royal Dutch Airlines (UK)

leavers or transferring someone from one department to another. The manager also generates the organisation charts and uses the spreadsheet for modelling.

The personnel assistant adds bulk operational data for employee records, e.g. sickness absence, ID card information, etc. She also looks after the word processing requirements and provides cover for the recruitment software.

The personnel manager at the Heathrow site is responsible for the electronic time-recording and roster-generation systems, and provides cover for the main personnel package, spreadsheet and selection testing software.

The personnel officer is responsible for the recruitment and selection systems and covers for the desk-top publishing and word processing packages.

The pensions officer looks after the in-house pension scheme.

Very sensibly the aim is to have each system covered by at least two trained staff in the department. This ensures that each area has a back-up and that operational knowledge is shared. But this shared ownership has also led to a significant improvement in morale within the department for the following reasons:

- Access to high-quality, realiable information
- Clear accountability within the department
- Mutual dependence on each other for core data
- Fast response to line manager questions – normally within five minutes
- Increased professionalism and IT awareness.

Corporate benefits

The marked improvement in HR effectiveness has had significant benefit to the company and its employees. The use of computer systems has enabled the department to cost justify many of the tasks it undertakes. These include both hard and soft benefits.

The more intangible soft benefits have included:

- The company and staff benefit from quick, accurate information.
- The company has been able to offer more sophisticated benefits to staff in the knowledge that these are administered efficiently with costs monitored and controlled.
- Use of electronic time-recording has allowed the company to introduce flexitime for dayworkers.
- Communication to staff is now more personal and professional, e.g. in terms of salary notification letters or appraisal forms.
- Over 4,000 job applications per year are handled efficiently (requiring approximately 10 per cent of personnel time, compared to the typical 60 per cent in most departments) and ensuring a guarantee to respond and process within 48 hours.
- Significant time savings allow the personnel function to spend more time on planning and implementing more imaginative and innovative policies.

But the department can also point to hard data showing improved benefits and savings. These include:

- Accurate, retrievable data in respect of manpower. Since staff costs account for 60 per cent of total operating costs within KLM UK, decisions can now be based on accurate data not guesswork. Furthermore, the department provides information within five minutes of request. The department is seen as a prime source of information by all levels of management.
- Monitoring an absence reduction scheme has shown that the programme costing £12,000 saved over £144,000 for the company (see example charts, Figures 6.3 and 6.4).

Figure 6.3

KLM absence reduction scheme – January 1992

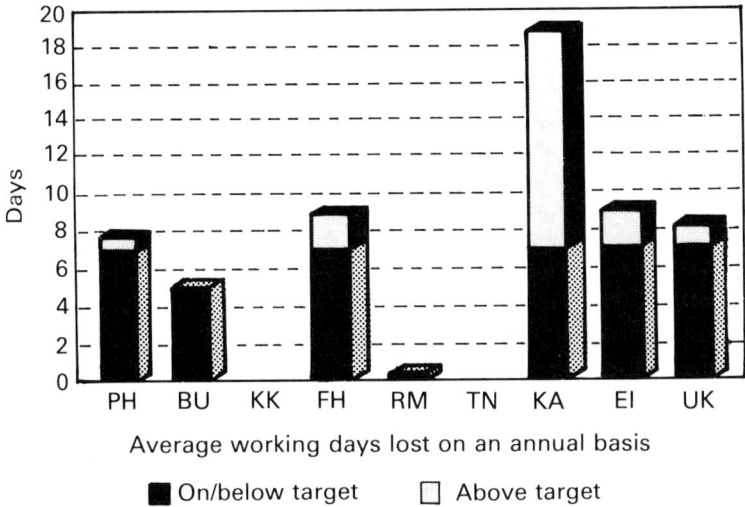

Average working days lost on an annual basis

■ On/below target   □ Above target

Reproduced with the permission of KLM Royal Dutch Airlines (UK)

- Use of the personnel assistant to provide in-house training on word processing has saved £20,000.
- Better selection and recruitment of staff through the use of computer-generated structured interviews.
- A saving of £400,000 in costs directly associated with the use of linked PC-based HR software packages. (Mainly through the rostering package.)
- The rostering package, with its links to both the personnel and payroll packages, ensures that the company makes full use of staff given the complex needs to match airline timetables. This has brought better use of resources plus a significant reduction in overtime/shift premia. Controlling costs can be immediate rather than waiting up to six weeks to investigate variances.
- Time-recording is now accurate and, again, immediate. Not only has this reduced an area of potential abuse but it

Figure 6.4

KLM absence reduction scheme – working days lost before
and since the introduction of the incentive scheme

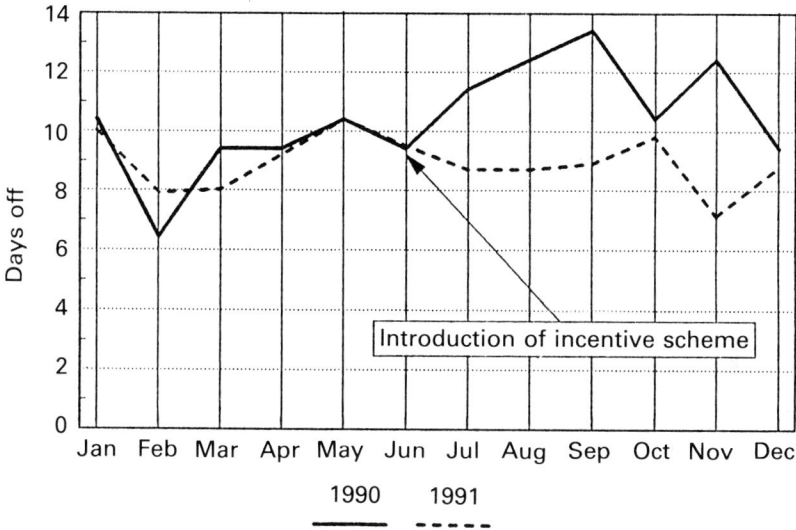

Reproduced with the permission of KLM Royal Dutch Airlines (UK)

has removed a 6 per cent error rate from the previous
manual system – and saved at least one man-year of work.

- Use of the computerised pension package has saved an
estimated £8,000 per annum in actuarial fees, plus giving
immediate information to employees.

The personnel manager believes that there is hardly anything
that HR people do which cannot be assisted by the use of
software. With so many specialist software programs now
available the key is to ensure that they mutually support and
share data. So much of personnel administration currently
involves unnecessary duplication.

He is also adamant that hands-on activity by senior personnel managers is vital. He estimates that he generally spends at

least three hours per day running reports and getting information from the system. The impact is that he is seen to be sharing workload with others in the department but, more significantly, other managers know that they can get an instant answer from anyone in the department. The credibility of the department is extremely high.

The use of IT systems has cut administrative time substantially and members of the department can now spend more time out and about with managers and employees. This has meant the department is more actively communicating with its clients – whether career counselling, advising on pension benefits, or supplying information and advice.

The success of the department in achieving HR administrative effectiveness has led to other European operations of KLM introducing the packages for their HR departments. It is a clear example of having information at your fingertips – quite literally.

7

▓ Effective Reward Management at Glaxo Pharmaceuticals UK

One of the key activities within human resources is compensation and benefits. In many cases this can mean monitoring and maintaining existing job evaluation structures; for most, it is a matter of undertaking salary and benefit research to ensure the company is broadly competitive.

Yet compensation and benefit management are critical to all organisations. Today's HR function needs to ensure not only that compensation meets the traditional needs to recruit, retain and motivate but also that increases in total remuneration are affordable and reflect real improvements in productivity and profit.

Background

Glaxo Pharmaceuticals is the UK subsidiary of Glaxo Holding plc – the world's second largest pharmaceutical company. The company sells and markets ethical pharmaceuticals. It employs 1,800 staff at two main sites based at Heathrow and Speke, Merseyside, and operates a nationwide sales force. Employees are largely non-unionised, professional or managerial staff.

Previous reward structure

The old reward system was based on over 14 grades covering all types of job. Within managerial grades there were no formal salary ranges and individuals 'progressed' by merit pay awards. For other staff the formal salary ranges had fallen into disrepute. Awards were made through a combination of 'cost of living' (RPI) and merit awards. In reality, long service had meant many were at top of grade, and continued corporate success meant that it became increasingly hard to fund increases from the merit pot.

There had been some attempt to set objectives during the annual appraisal. But this was not consistent across all areas. As a result, the reward system had limited ability to recognise performance, there was little incentive for training or personal development, and there was no recognition of market differentials between different job groups.

Creating a new structure

The company set three objectives for any new structure. These were:

- To measure and reward individual performance in a fair manner by clear objective setting in appraisals
- To provide career progression and reward acquisition of skills and knowledge
- To ensure salaries remained market competitive.

These aims were met by moving to a reward structure based on job families, where performance ratings are matched against a series of proficiency levels.

The objective-setting process has been co-ordinated to ensure that individual objectives tie in to role, departmental and corporate objectives and that all of these are consistent with the corporate five-year operating plans as shown in the Figure 7.1.

Performance appraisal is assessed against six categories. This was deliberately chosen to avoid any middle level so managers are forced to make and justify a selection. Second, the category labels are not numbered 1 to 6 or A to F as these have connotations with educational qualifications. The categories are:

Figure 7.1
The objective-setting process

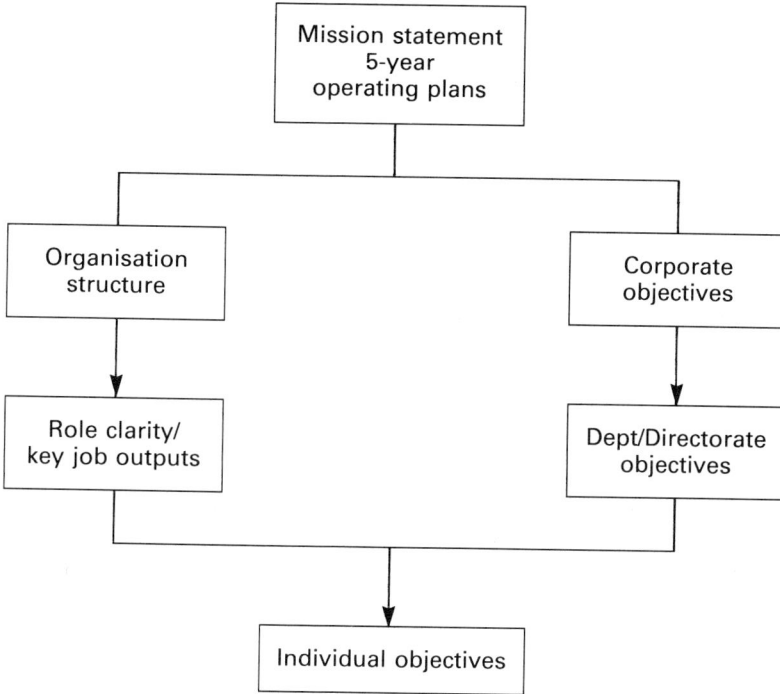

Reproduced with the permission of Glaxo Pharmaceuticals UK

O Outstanding overall performance
E Excellent overall performance
G Good overall performance
S Satisfactory overall performance
R Overall performance requires improvement
U Unacceptable overall performance

For each category there is a clear description provided as a guideline to both managers and employees. For example, to achieve Level G, a person needs to have met *all* their key objectives and over achieved in one or two objectives.

The second element was to move to broad job families. A job family is defined as a group of jobs with similar skills, knowledge and output. Examples of job families are:

- Field sales
- Computer operators
- Secretarial
- Administration.

This allows more flexibility and mobility across the organisation and also emphasises team structures.

Proficiency levels

Within each job family a number of proficiency levels have been set up. Individuals progress through the steps within the job family by acquiring greater skill and knowledge, greater experience, or by taking on more complex responsibilities. As with appraisal levels each step has a level description.

The number of levels varies with job family, for example the sales group has three levels, marketing has two and IT five. Most have three and these can be seen as a training or developmental stage, a core stage and an advanced stage. This therefore provides a means of progression within job families, over and above performance measurement. In the past, rewarding progression was lost in subjective performance assessment.

Matching market salaries

The third element in the reward structure is the need to ensure that salary levels are competitive in the marketplace. This is obtained through salary survey at three levels:

- Local salary survey club
- Pharmaceutical salary surveys

Figure 7.2

Six pay curves, matching performance appraisal categories

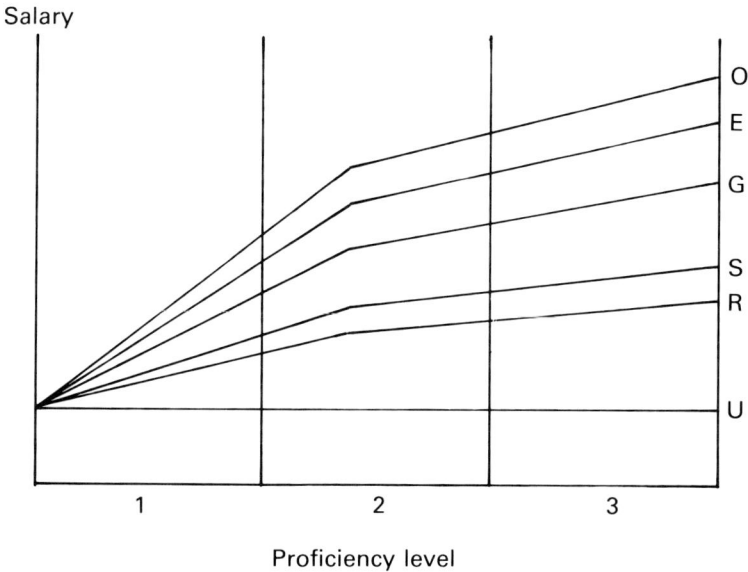

Reproduced with the permission of Glaxo Pharmaceuticals UK

- Functional salary surveys.

These data establish a base level for each job family and there are six pay curves for each job family to match the performance appraisal categories as shown in Figure 7.2. The pay curves are reviewed annually and guidelines issued to line managers.

The structure then applies the proficiency levels within the pay curves for the relevant job family. Managers can now match salary to performance, market rate and role proficiency (see Figure 7.3).

The process is dynamic, so a person may achieve a higher rating in one year than the next, although for most staff there is more likely to be general progression. For those who have a

Figure 7.3
Matching salary to performance, market rate and role
proficiency

Salary

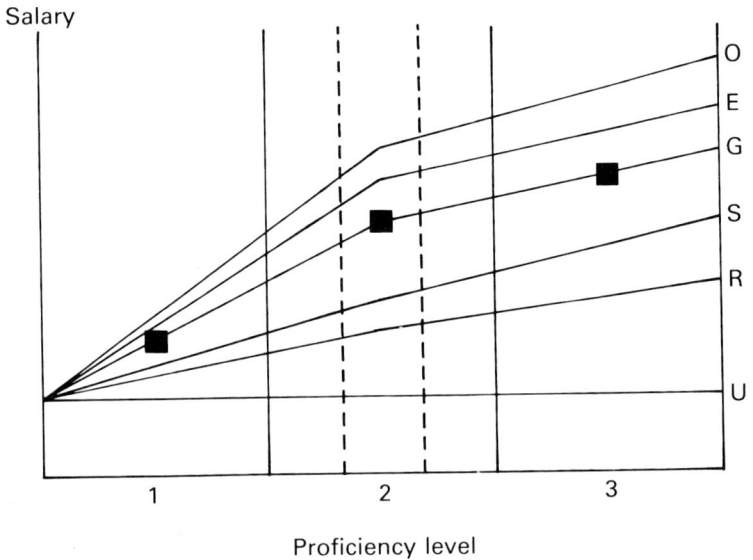

Proficiency level

Reproduced with the permission of Glaxo Pharmaceuticals UK

lower rating one year *vis-à-vis* another, a rolling average is
applied so that relative salary falls are cushioned.

Implementation

To both change the basis of pay and ensure the system is
owned by line managers, the HR function had to provide
considerable training to managers and effective communication to all employees. Managers, in particular, needed to be
reassured that the reward structure would be an effective,
additional tool. Employees needed to be reassured that the
system would introduce greater fairness in performance

appraisal, and would provide more training and employee development opportunities.

The HR function could only implement such a structure with computer support, partly to plot the relevant pay curves and also to monitor potential salary drift.

Furthermore, the company has closely monitored the objective setting and performance rating by line managers. By reviewing these ratings in manager's workshops, the company has achieved greater consistency and awareness among the managers.

Does it work?

The scheme was introduced in 1990 and to date it has been successful. Pay is now based on a mix of performance and proficiency rather than cost of living and dubious merit awards. Performance appraisal is now implemented throughout the company against a set of consistent criteria. Objective setting has become more focused to business needs and hence corporate performance.

The company has also found a way of rewarding learning and development so individuals are encouraged to acquire skills, knowledge and experience. The structure also ensures that market data can be incorporated into the pay structure, thereby matching external relativities to internal needs.

But has it improved performance? This is harder to gauge. Glaxo Pharmaceuticals is one of the highest-performing subsidiaries in a high-performing organisation. Consequently, it is harder to pinpoint specific contributions to improved performance. The HR function is, however, convinced that the new structure has helped maintain performance levels and has created a new climate where jobs and pay are focused on delivering results.

8

Competency Modelling and Skill Profiling at Bull UK

This case study illustrates how an ambitious radical shift in both HR practice and corporate development can be achieved. The programme covers the entire organisation. Two key elements of the initiative are the formation of a company-wide training and development function within the human resources section (combining previously functionally aligned training sections), plus the use of an advanced software program which allows the company to carry out job skill profiling and employee assessment. This 'expert system' allows employees to complete their own self-assessment against a defined job profile and to compare this with that of their manager. The impact of this initiative has been to ally HR closely with corporate business goals, and to allow the department to assess the perceived skill gap against assessed and required competency levels.

Background

Bull Information Systems developed from the former Information Systems Division of Honeywell Inc., with the French state-owned Groupe Bull taking a 42.5 per cent share of the joint company in 1987 and then acquiring the company the following year.

Honeywell Information Systems in the UK was a company offering a full range of products specialising in mainframe and minisystems to Government, local government and major corporates. With the transition from hardware to software markets, plus the rise of end-user computing, there was a radical shift from computer manufacturing to 'solution' supply – where the company sought to provide hardware and software centred around Open System technology, plus associated consultancy and support services.

Groupe Bull has operations throughout Europe and America. Within the UK the company has 16 offices employing over 1,900 people. While there is a small manufacturing presence, the employees are primarily involved in engineering and customer services (600), systems integration (480), and sales and marketing (approximately 300).

Changing the business focus

Bull has seen radical change, largely through a major technological switch, demanding both substantial recruitment and retraining. More significantly there has also been a need to refocus the sales group given the strategic change from selling to IT/MIS professionals to the targeting of end-user client groups. The 'solution' sale, with its emphasis on service and results, is now aimed at chief executives and operational directors.

Like many companies, Bull Information Systems had built a hierarchical management structure with rigid empires based on a small number of broad sales sectors (government, public sector and commercial sales). But with privatisation within some sections of the public sector, and pressure elsewhere to adopt competitive tendering and value-for-money purchasing, Bull has found that these traditional markets have come under increasing commercial pressure. Rapid technological developments and the move to Open Systems has added to the challenge facing the company.

To succeed the company required a flatter, flexible structure based on appropriate skills and the ability to match client requirements. The rise of end-user computing has also demanded guaranteed service standards for support. As a result, support and technical staff needed to be incorporated within individual project teams.

In addition, the matrix needed to be three-dimensional with

the link combining sales, support and corporate administrative staff. This is represented in Figure 8.1. To achieve this change required a fundamental shift in emphasis from direct reports to teamworking.

Working together in teams

To encourage co-operation and development of teams, the company set up a college programme involving a series of two-day residential courses throughout the UK. Over 600 staff attended these workshops to highlight the new corporate values. Key to this was a need to ensure line management was more proactive through devolved responsibility.

But behind all these moves has been a need to ensure that the new matrix/team-based structure is customer-driven.

On-going development

Fundamental in the construction of project teams is a clear understanding of both the existing and required skill base. This demands identification of 'what the key skills for the organisation are'. Bull UK used assessment centres to identify some of the key skills required by its new strategic direction, notably strategic analysis, critical thinking, creativity and risk. But this method did not provide information about technological and operational skills.

The company recognises that no model in today's economic climate can be static – it must evolve to combine essential manpower planning in order to respond to change.

Skill profiling

Considerable investment has been made in qualifying the skill gap. The training and development team, with other HR professionals, looked to identify the key skills and competen-

Figure 8.1
Three-dimensional teamwork model

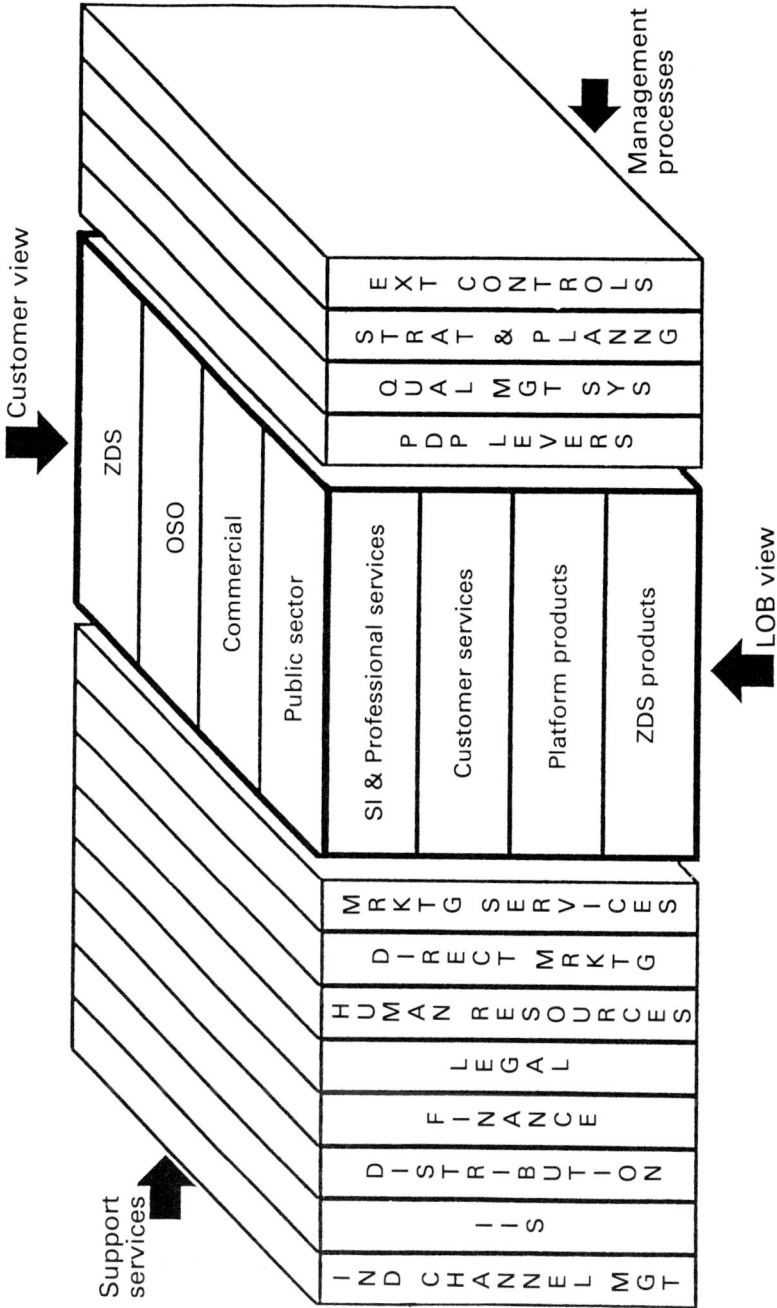

Customer view

Management processes

ZDS

OSO

Commercial

Public sector

SI & Professional services

Customer services

Platform products

ZDS products

EXT CONTROLS

STRAT & PLANNG

QUAL MGT SYS

PDP LEVERS

MRKTG SERVICES

DIRECT MRKTG

HUMAN RESOURCES

LEGAL

FINANCE

DISTRIBUTION

IIS

IND CHANNEL MGT

Support services

LOB view

cies both within existing staff and those needed by the business. This meant incorporating attitudinal competencies such as 'drive and enthusiasm' as well as technical and professional skills.

The aim was to create a framework whereby business results could be overlaid to ask 'why did a particular team succeed?'. From this, core competencies can be developed for given roles.

Use of expert system software

Bull selected the software package PEODESY which provides an employee records and training administration system but also includes an expert system capability for job skills profiling. Through this facility users can establish skill profiles for generic and specific jobs. The profiles are built up through structured question and answer sessions (job analysis), where the user is asked to describe the responsibilities and function of the job in question. The software draws inferences from the responses and produces a job profile in terms of essential and desirable skill attributes held within its skills knowledge database.

The skill attributes, job analysis questions and inferences have been tailored and modified to meet Bull's requirements. This has been where much of the work has been spent (in terms of time and money) in the development of the project.

Bull believes that the choice of an expert system has been critical to the project, giving significant advantages over manual methods:

- *Objectivity*. By deriving skill profiles from questions related to job function and responsibility, employees and managers (the system users) are forced to concentrate on the job function while the knowledge base within the software builds up the skill profile.
- *Flexibility*. Skill attributes can be added and the knowledge amended to respond to the changing requirements of the organisation.

- *Accessibility*. During 1993, all managers gained on-line access to the system from their desks, and employees became able to perform self-assessment against a given job profile, compare this assessment with that of their manager and, by so doing, obtain advice concerning necessary training and development activity.
- *Detail*. The skill profiling is in considerable detail. At present the non-technical skill database (i.e. covering sales and marketing jobs) has over 90 skill attributes identified.

A full evaluation session for a single or generic job takes approximately 20 to 40 minutes.

For the technical skills, the wide nature of technical products provided by both Bull and third-party suppliers now supported by Bull means that the problem of identifying relevant skill attributes has been more complex. Generic technical skills and product specific skills have been separated. Programming ability, fault diagnosis, problem-solving, etc. have been defined as 'generic' skills, with product specific competencies added as a separate database component.

Defining generic jobs

Clearly it was not feasible to attempt to build skill profiles for all discrete job titles across the company. Instead a series of broad generic jobs have been mapped with matrices dividing jobs into a series of 'job cells'. For sales positions, jobs are categorised by job function (sales consultant, specialist sales executive, business unit manager, etc.) and by the type of accounts for which they are responsible (major accounts, new names, etc.), as shown in Figure 8.2.

Similarly, marketing jobs have been segmented by marketing consultant and marketing manager against areas of responsibility (total product/brand management, product specialist, marketing promotions, etc.), as shown in Figure 8.3.

For each generic job cell a minimum of three people have

Figure 8.2

Matrix categorising sales positions by job function and by type of account

Job function	Major accounts	General accounts	New name accounts	Line of business/ specialist
Sales professional	A	B	C	D
	Major accounts & vertical market	General accounts	New name accounts	Line of business/ specialist
Business unit manager/ Sales manager	E	F	G	H

Figure 8.3

Matrix categorising marketing positions by job function and by area of responsibility

Job function	Total product/ brand management	Product management	Programmes management	Public affairs	Business planning
Marketing pro- fessional	I	J	K	L	M
	Marketing & business development			Public affairs	Business planning
Line manager	N			O	P

completed a job analysis session to build a profile for the job. In most cases this has been done by two job holders and one manager. Input has also been sought from one other manager who has detailed knowledge of the job. In this way the job skill profiles have been compared and a consensus profile agreed. The output forms the basic skill profile on the software for jobs falling within that job cell. With use, all the skill profiles will be continually updated.

Operational impact

One of the first changes has been the incorporation of skills assessment within the appraisal process (currently annual, but more frequent appraisal is planned). Employees are encouraged to regularly review their own skill profiles to ensure that their personal details are kept up to date.

The skill database now means that a project manager can select the appropriate individual for a particular job, and the organisation can make full use of all available talent and experience.

The software being used provides a succession planning module which can give the closest match to requirements in most situations against five distinct levels (ranging from none to limited to expert status).

As detailed in the Edmund Nuttall case study (see Chapter 9), this now means that proposals and tenders can include examples of CV experience of the team to work on a given project, and this is seen to give competitive advantage where service and the match to client requirements is the main commercial criterion.

Every manager (including project managers) has direct access to the employee database and the skill sets. The system is regularly updated by both individual employees and line managers. In this respect the traditional personnel system has been superseded by an on-line information resource.

How has this been achieved?

The project was introduced via a high level steering group which sought the views of line managers; two groups of 20 managers and professional staff were asked to identify the critical skills for the organisation.

The next stage was to relaunch staff appraisal under the banner of staff development, but which included greater emphasis on coaching, motivation and competency evaluation. This required a three-day training course for managers.

The project also led to increased centralisation of training but this is seen as a temporary step in order to co-ordinate the database. The aim will be to return the delivery of training and development to local teams.

Furthermore, the project demanded that a corporate training plan was prepared for the first time but significantly this was dovetailed into the HR and business plans. The training plan for 1993 presented seven key objectives to the board, focusing on management and technical development. This has been endorsed by the board through its commitment to:

- Setting a strategic sales direction
- The management of people

as the fundamental planks of corporate strategy.

In stressing the importance of managing people, the company has emphasised the cost of investing in people. It has now set its sights on achieving management level NVQs and the Investor In People (IIP) award.

Judging effectiveness

In this case study how might we gauge the effectiveness of the programme? The first and crucial indicator is that the HR department has allied its activity to the very heart of the business and the need to be responsive to the customer. This is translated as ensuring project teams have the best skills and experience available to meet customer requirements.

It has also delivered a service directly to the line management. The department has sought to provide on-line access to employee information, and in doing so has raised the quality and relevance of information supplied. The main benefit of this has been that HR staff can now reallocate their time, with a significant shift in priorities geared to developing the business.

Both the information and activities of the department have become more strategic, with plans co-ordinated with both manpower and business planning. It is also more forward-thinking in that planning is now taking place well in advance of implementation.

The role of Personnel has now changed. The department is no longer largely administrative; it sees itself as proactive. Personnel has become the internal consultant advising line managers on best practice since managers now have direct access to relevant information. Just as the organisation has changed radically to focus on the needs of the market, so too the department now tries to think 'customer' in dealing with corporate colleagues.

The real test is whether managers and employees make full use of the potential.

9

♟ Building a Quality Service – Edmund Nuttall's Experience

This case study shows how leadership plus a need to satisfy local managers helped change a personnel function from being largely administrative to being a proactive support for the business. By adopting a quest for quality and responsiveness to clients, the department has gained respect, pride and justified its role in helping to shape the development of the organisation.

Background

Edmund Nuttall Limited is an established firm of civil engineering contractors with over 125 years' experience. It specialises in the construction of complex, multi-million-pound civil engineering projects across the world. These include building dams, roads, tunnels, bridges and harbours. Its hallmark has been 'engineering excellence' where quality is the key criterion. Much of its work is carried out to BS 5750/ISO 9000 standards.

The company employs approximately 1,500 people, with nine regional offices throughout the UK. Each office is headed by a regional director or area manager. They in turn are responsible for the successful completion of major projects being undertaken at over 50 sites.

Each site is a large civil engineering project with a value of between £10m and £25m, but some are worth £100m or more. Not surprisingly, each project can be considered a business in its own right. The project manager or director has similar responsibilities to any general manager or managing director running their own business. The problem, however, is that this person needs to relocate and start up again every two or three years, as one project finishes and another begins. And each time it is likely to be with a different management team and associated specialists including designers, planners, estimators, engineers, quantity surveyors, etc.

The demands of each project, of course, vary markedly. Consequently, any new project needs careful matching of appropriate skills and experience. This requires detailed records and thorough appraisal.

Although well established, Nuttall's recent expansion has occurred since joining the Dutch HBG construction group. This has meant that the company has moved from a centralised, 'family' business to a highly decentralised organisation. This expansion, which meant the company doubled in size over a relatively short period, also prompted the need to review management structures, systems, procedures and operating style.

The human resource function

This had grown over the years to a group of ten people – each with a great deal of experience in a given area, e.g. personnel administration, pensions, payroll, training, etc. And, of course, each kept their own sets of records.

Not surprisingly this meant trying to collect and analyse information from these sections was a problem. Each request seemed to be a major exercise in its own right. The service to the company and line managers was limited.

The need to audit

When the HR director was appointed, the first thing he did was to visit each of the regions and sites – partly to understand the business more clearly but also to find out what people required of the function. In essence the HR director undertook a detailed audit covering the following areas:

- Company culture
- Employee morale
- Communication
- Career development
- Training and development
- Industrial relations
- Manpower resourcing
- Remuneration.

But most important of all, he asked line managers 'what support, help and service they needed from the human resource function to help them manage their part of the business better.'

The audit exercise meant that an action plan could be put together which set out specific short-term targets (within the first 18 months) and some longer-term goals.

The four key short-term goals were:

1 To get board agreement to a policy statement detailing the 'Role of the Human Resources Function'. This would establish a framework for the department and provide line management with a clear understanding of what the function should and would provide.
2 To ensure that the personnel, training and pensions departments were resourced with competent staff who understood the needs of the business.
3 To establish comprehensive personnel, training and pensions records together with associated systems and procedures.
4 To build up the credibility of the human resource function.

The need for accurate and comprehensive records was fundamental. High levels of commitment and hard work by the human resource team could not compensate for poor or inadequate information. The director recognised that the function could only become an influential force within the senior management team if it could back up its proposals with facts – hunches and feelings were not enough.

The medium-term plans included a need to review or introduce:

- Regular performance review
- Job grading
- Improved project resourcing
- Manpower planning
- Training provision
- Management development
- Salary and benefit planning.

But before these could be implemented, the HR director wanted human resources to be seen as a function that would help the business succeed and make a profit. He believed that it was essential that the function must provide a good day-to-day service for line managers first before attempting to win credibility for more creative and pioneering initiatives.

The immediate plan was simple. All short-term effort was to be devoted to: 'Creating a unified, accurate and up-to-date records system that could provide a wide variety of easily read information relatively quickly.'

Implementing the plan

The first priority was to identify software which could store all personnel, training and pensions information, and equally important would allow easy access to the information and generate reports that would be easy to read. But these reports were not intended solely for the HR departments. The priority was to provide reports for the line managers.

Having selected the software, the function then turned its attention to 'systems and procedures'. Many of the existing procedures were in different people's heads. The team set about getting the information out of the heads and onto paper. A working party was established which met for half a day every week for six weeks. This was extremely demanding but the team was convinced that the job would only get done with this level of commitment. It would not succeed on an 'as and when' basis.

The workload was split into a number of logical sections, for example:

- Pre-employment
- During employment
- Remuneration
- Pensions
- Private medical care
- Termination of employment.

Taking each in turn, the team asked: what happens? Which forms are used? Who does what? Where are the forms passed onto? The answers to these questions enabled the team to prepare flowcharts for each operation showing clearly who did what and which forms were used. At the same time the working party reviewed the effectiveness of each form by asking:

- Did the form provide the information required?
- Was it quick and easy to complete?

The team needed to take care since most forms were completed by others outside the department and there was also a real danger of creating a paperwork mountain.

The working party reviewed all the various forms – many of somewhat dubious origin – and designed a revised company format to apply to all forms. This helped to give a consistent identity. But the main objective was to make them easy to complete and to convey a professional quality image of the company and the human resource department to internal and external clients (i.e. managers, employees and applicants alike).

The outcome was a two-part manual:

- Part 1, comprising some 52 flowcharts documenting the administrative procedures of HR.
- Part 2, comprising some 92 standard forms and letters following the new quality format.

Once everybody in the department had been briefed, the next stage was to brief and sell it to the line.

The team prepared a slimmed down version for use by the regional, area and site offices. Indeed the HR director took this further by preparing expanding file packs with a summary of personnel procedures together with supplies of all the relevant forms that managers would require, e.g. job application forms, staff transfer forms, salary change notifications, subsistence allowance applications, company car requests, etc.

The director then set off around the regions and sites once again, to brief area managers on the revised procedures, explain why the changes had been made, and to provide them with what he describes as their 'Personnel Starter Pack'.

Managing the information

With a person dedicated to get the computer software up and running, the department loaded all relevant data and asked employees to update the records held on file. This was to ensure accuracy of the base data.

Additional data was identified through the working party review of the various systems and procedures, e.g. the data necessary to maintain pensions, life assurance, private health and payroll. As a result the necessary internal reports were specified.

The HR director took personal responsibility for identifying the necessary reports required by the function's clients – the directors and line managers. But these were not general wish lists but specific replies to the question: What information would help you manage the business more effectively?

The format of reports was made a key consideration. They had to be relevant and easy to read. Draft report layouts were tested to ensure information was in the right place, the right order and in 'English' – not coded jargon. Emphasis was rightly placed on producing high-quality presentation.

Some of these reports can be shown to have direct impact on the company's profitability. For example:

1 *Company Employment History*. This report is like a mini-CV which provides a one-page overview of an employee's experience together with the names of the various managers for whom the person has worked. Previously this could only be achieved by time-consuming search through manual files.

   This report, now quickly generated through the computer, is proving to be one of the most important reports because it is not only used for project resourcing but also is valuable in presenting bids and winning business.

2 *Staff Development Report*. An annual staff performance review was re-launched in 1992. Previously this had become a 'box ticking' exercise. Much of the credibility of such meetings had been lost in the past when managers and employees realised that agreed training had not been undertaken from the previous review.

   To overcome the problem, staff development reports are now prepared for each individual job holder and his manager giving details of:

   • All training undertaken since joining the company
   • Names of reviewing managers
   • What training plans were agreed
   • What development plans were agreed.

   As a result the job holder is now able to progress his or her

Figure 9.1
The format of Edmund Nuttall's Quality Management System

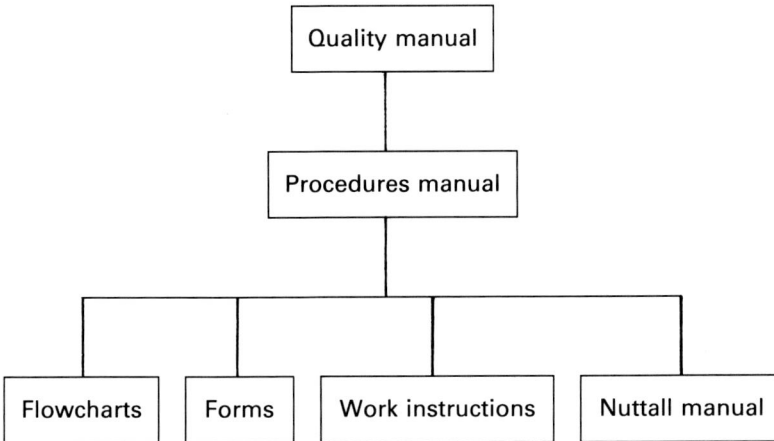

Reproduced with the permission of Edmund Nuttall Ltd

own training and development, while the manager is aware
of obligations of recommending and monitoring agreed
training.

3 *Cost Centre Reports*. This report is produced each month
for the regional director/area manager. It provides up-to-
date information on who is on which project and also allows
the manager to monitor the subsistence and lodging allowance expenditure.

Preparing a quality manual

In addition the function has used its preparation of the Systems
and Procedures Manuals to document to BS 5750 standard.
The department has now established a Quality Management
System, the format of which is illustrated in Figure 9.1

Quality policy

As part of its submission in respect of BS 5750 Part 1, the quality policy of the function is declared as follows:

> . . . to ensure that the agreed quality standards are met throughout all phases of contribution to company strategy.
>
> Function strategy is to work with management to create a company organisation and culture in which people are committed to the success of the business, understand the importance of their job and seek continuous improvement of their own and their team's performance.
>
> The Director, Human Resources has overall responsibility for Quality Assurance and Quality Control. . . . The Director, Human Resources is nominated as the Management Representative for Quality with responsibility for effective operation of the Quality System. All Human Resource staff, however, have a responsibility for quality and are required to conform to the procedures referred to in this manual. Staff are encouraged to inform their Manager of any changes which could improve quality.
>
> The procedures referred to in this manual have been introduced for the purpose of achieving sound operational and quality practices within the Function. Such procedures conform to the requirements of BS 5750: Part 1 and are the minimum standards adopted.

Objectives of the quality system

In setting the context for the quality system, the Quality Manual defines the following objectives:

> *4.1   Human Resources and Objectives*
> In order that the Company's objectives may be achieved the Human Resources Function objectives include:
> 4.1.1   Attract, motivate, develop and retain high calibre people.
> 4.1.2   Build effective organisations and teams.
> 4.1.3   Provide an efficient service to line management.

4.2   Quality System Objectives

4.2.1   Maintain pre-determined levels of quality for all services and products provided.

4.2.2   Detect and improve areas of unsatisfactory quality.

4.2.3   Provide a documented reference system for the Quality Management System.

4.2.4   Provide an internal training scheme to ensure that all Human Resources staff can adequately achieve the objectives of the Function's Quality Policy.

4.2.5   Provide evidence of the existence of those policies and procedures.

4.2.6   Ensure that the Quality Policy and operation procedures are properly communicated to the appropriate staff.

The benefits of the programme

The two extracts above clearly illustrate the commitment to the client in terms of service levels, the need for documentation and responsibilities within the department.

This programme has been highly successful. At one level the HR director has established:

- A team of human resource people who now understand more clearly that their job is to support and help the operation.
- A team who know what is expected of them.
- Company human resource systems and procedures that are clear, concise and are understood both in the field and at Head Office.
- An effective computerised personnel information system with on-line access to eight people in the department.

But at a more important level:

- Operational management see the human resource function supporting them.

- Better HR information is now helping management in the control of its costs.
- Better HR information is helping with project resourcing, i.e. fitting experience and skills to the needs of individual projects.
- Better HR information is helping line management with the training and development of their staff.
- Operational management are gaining confidence in the HR function and are increasingly turning to them for help and guidance.

10

♟ Concluding Remarks

Personnel in transition

Many within the profession express concern at the pace of change occurring around them and anxiety in their ability to act effectively. Some see their departments under threat as organisations look to slim down indirect staff. Indeed, for some the pressure is so great that Personnel has been asked to lead the way in shedding resources.

In addition, attention to de-layering, process re-engineering and lean production has demanded effective empowerment of first line managers/team leaders. As Personnel helps implement such policies, it is understandably uneasy as it relinquishes traditional HR areas – e.g. absence, training and appraisal – to the line. The function needs to change. It is no longer the administration or welfare department; many of its sacred cows such as job evaluation, recruitment and selection are under review. Its character is changing but many have yet to alter the culture, both within the team, and employee and manager perceptions of the function.

Senior personnel management talk about the function's role as a facilitator whereby Personnel is concerned with creating a new environment which enables line management to recruit, train and motivate employees today and for the future. But in many cases the department needs to unite its own team to accommodate such a role.

Others have talked about Personnel acting as an 'internal consultancy' – a source of excellence. But in what? For many working within Personnel this sense of purpose has yet to be defined and communicated to the rest of the organisation. As a result many departments are giving off conflicting signals and communicating mixed accountability.

As the Lead Body on Personnel Standards has recognised, a number of conflicts need to be addressed:

- The degree of integration of personnel strategy into business plans
- Acceptance that ownership of people management lies with the line.
- The need to balance the business needs with 'best practice'.
- The need to establish accountability for the quality of service provided.

Furthermore, since the success (and in many cases the survival) of the business depends on the organisation's ability to improve continuously in a context of perpetual change, Personnel needs to firmly identify itself with these business challenges. These challenges are summarised as the need to:

- Innovate
- Improve quality
- Reduce costs and improve value
- Provide faster and more sensitive response to clients.

The pressure on the human resource department is growing. There is significant change in organisational structures as many companies move from functional hierarchies to smaller, more flexible business units. There is also the rising tide of mergers, acquisitions and joint ventures – all of which bring cultural change. Equally, companies are looking to take on European or international identities. These tend to create an impression of constant or semi-permament states of reorganisation.

There are also changes within the workforce. For example, the greater proportion of women contributing to the skills and experience available to the business; changing attitudes towards long-term careers with given employers; and the marked impact of new technology.

With so much potential change, the personnel function needs to be operating with maximum efficiency – but efficiency alone is not enough. Energy needs to be channelled into the areas supporting the business goals: thus effectiveness demands an understanding of the business strategy and getting close to operational management. Personnel therefore needs to be client focused.

HR audits will become standard

The measurement of HR activity is likely to become a necessary, on-going activity for the majority of personnel departments. Auditing is an accepted part of business management. As organisations look to maximise their investment in human resources they will seek closer controls on spending. The importance of budgeting and cost-benefit analysis of personnel activity, notably training and management development, will lead to a growing demand for new ways of documenting, costing and monitoring the work of the department.

Quality initiatives will also result in regular monitoring of activity and, as highlighted in Chapter 4, are a fundamental condition of assessment. Once such initiatives are established, Personnel will more widely appreciate the benefit of benchmarking and statistical control as a way of demonstrating performance and identifying areas for improvement. If HR practitioners are going to justify their role in terms of 'value-added' or 'contributions to the bottom-line', they will need to establish relevant methods of measurement.

The HR audit also has wider benefits. It helps the function to establish its current position, assess the needs and therefore identify actions required. It therefore helps to set the agenda for the development of the function and assign priorities.

There are two important warnings: first, the department must be prepared to take action on the results; and second, in drawing up an action plan, care needs to taken not to over-commit. If resources are not available, a step-by-step improvement programme will help ensure a series of small successes.

The need to unlock IT potential

Most departments have some form of computerisation. But few are realising its potential. On average, I would estimate only 20 per cent are utilising their computerised personnel systems to any significant degree. In many cases the lack of general IT training in databases and associated graphics severely limits the department's ability to deliver quality information. The case studies of KLM, Edmund Nuttall and Glaxo illustrate the gains which can be made (see Chapters 6, 9 and 7).

IT provides the means of access, response and quality in presentation. A small investment can reap major benefits both in terms of improved efficiency and credibility. For many it seems the original aims and justifications have withered through lack of direction and nurture.

Clear relevant procedures

Effectiveness is directly linked to the relevance and usefulness of personnel procedures. These should not be presented as rules but as the way to maximise resources, reduce duplication and ensure a speedy response. By being given clear operational advice, managers should be able to make most decisions as to necessary action without additional consultation or delay. The prime requirement is that procedures need to be simple, be easy to follow and reduce paperflow.

Involvement and communication

If personnel staff are to be effective as consultants or facilitators, they need to ensure a communications strategy is in place. Such a role requires high trust, integrity and openness. One danger is that Personnel can become everybody's client and therefore commitments cannot be open-ended.

Personnel needs to market itself better and needs to manage expectations. Too often I hear criticism of intitiatives which are viewed as 'the flavour of the month' simply because employees were not given a broad time frame for implementation. As a result, some fail to materialise because line management has not known what to expect and has not reacted. If personnel solutions are to be owned by the line, operational management needs to be actively involved in the design. Commitment must be won prior to implementation.

Achieving HR effectiveness

This book has hopefully given some insight into the way to review your operations plus case study material of leading organisations who have won the respect and credibility of their organisations and others in the personnel field.

There is no set formula. Each organisation's personnel function will differ in character, style and culture. If these meet the organisation's needs, the department can be said to be effective but it will still need to review and adapt to ever-changing requirements.

To be seen to be effective, the department should attempt to answer the following questions:

1 Who will judge the success of the function?
2 What changes are affecting our organisation and are we prepared for them?
3 What key results will reflect our contribution to the business?

There are five characteristics which are most evident in effective personnel departments:

- They are highly responsive – putting the client first.
- They are seen to be very professional (especially in terms of output or presentation).
- They have high respect at all levels.
- They operate as one team.
- They are committed to improving the quality of the service provided.

By pursuing a goal of improved effectiveness, there is considerable payback to the organisation, to the department and to individuals. There is enhanced credibility and hence self-confidence, greater professionalism, raised morale, better teamwork, and the challenge of success – as one organisation described it, 'learning to win'.

♟ Suggested Reading

Books

ARMSTRONG, M. *Strategies for human resource management: a total business approach*, London, Kogan Page, 1992

COLLARD, R. *Total quality: success through people*, London, IPM, 1993 (2nd Edition)

COLLINS, M. *Human resources management audit – North Western and West Midlands Health Authorities*, North-Western and West Midlands Health Authorities, Birmingham, 1991

CONNOCK, S. *HR Vision*, London, IPM, 1991

CROSBY, P. *Completeness: quality for the 21st century*, New York, Dutton, 1992

ERNST & YOUNG *Total quality: a manager's guide for the 1990s*, Kogan Page, 1992

FITZ-ENZ, J. *How to measure human resource management*, New York, McGraw Hill, 1984

INSTITUTE OF PERSONNEL MANAGEMENT *Quality: people management matters*, Research series, London, IPM, 1993

LYNCH, J. *Making manpower more effective*, London, Pan Books, 1982

PERSONNEL STANDARDS LEAD BODY *A perspective on personnel*, London, HMSO, 1993

TYSON, S. and FELL, A. *Evaluating the personnel function*, Cheltenham, Stanley Thornes, 1992 (2nd Edition)

Articles

BILES, G. 'Auditing HRM practices: is your department contributing as much to the organisation as it could?', *Personnel Administrator* (USA), Vol. 31 No. 12, December 1986, pp. 89–90, 92, 94

BOWEN, D. and LAWLER, E. 'Total quality human resources management', *Organizational Dynamics* (USA), Vol. 20 No. 4, Spring 1992, p. 29–41

BURN, and THOMPSON, L. 'When personnel calls in the auditors', *Personnel Management*, Vol. 25 No. 1, January 1993, pp. 28–31

Employee Development Bulletin, 'BS 5750 quality registration for

ICL's training function', IR–RR No. 528, Industrial Relations Services, EDB pp. 10–14

Employment Digest, 'Auditing personnel procedures and policies', No. 184, July 1985, pp. 4–5

FOWLER, A. 'What is the value of personnel departments?', *Local Government Chronicle*, No. 6246, March 1987, p. 14

FOWLER, A., WIBBERLEY, M. and SHEARD, M. 'Two routes to quality', *Personnel Management*, Vol. 24 No. 11, November 1992, pp. 30–34

MARCHINGTON, M., WILKINSON, A. and DALE, B. 'Who is really taking the lead on quality?' *Personnel Management*, Vol. 25 No. 4, April 1993, pp. 30–33

MATTHEWMAN, J. 'Introducing quality into personnel', *Employment Digest*, No 338, July 1992, pp. 4–6

MATTHEWMAN J. 'Auditing the personnel function', *Employment Digest*, No. 349, February 1993, pp. 1–3

MOYNIHAN, E. 'BS 5750 and payroll administration', *Payroll Manager's Review*, Vol. 7 No. 3, January 1993, pp. 22–23

RILEY, K. and SLOMAN, M. 'Milestones for the personnel department', *Personnel Management*, Vol. 23 No. 8, August 1991, pp. 34–37

SEGAL, J. and QUINN, M. 'How to audit your HR programs', *Personnel Administrator* (USA), Vol. 34 No. 5, May 1989, pp. 67–70

Index

absence
 monitoring 20–21, 22, 23, 43
  packages used by KLM 101,
   103–5
 policy audit 34
acquisitions and mergers 136
 by ICL 79–80, 81
appraisal systems
 audit 34
 Bull UK 121, 122
 Edmund Nuttall Ltd 130–31
 Glaxo Pharmaceuticals UK
  108–9, 111, 112
 ICL 90–91
assessment centres 116
audits see HR audits

benchmarking 12, 42–4, 82–3, 137
boards of directors
 commitment to quality
  framework 51–2, 126
 personnel representation on 7–8
bonus schemes 92, 93
Bosch 63
British Standards Institution (BSI)
 64
 see also quality standards
Bull UK 114–123
business markets, changes in, for
 ICL 78, 80, 82
business strategy, and HR strategy
 8, 12–13, 15, 29–30, 54–6, 86,
 108, 109, 122–3, 136

career development 84
change
 cultural 17, 62, 78, 81, 82, 84–6,
  135, 136
 management of 11–14, 17, 29, 42,
  49
 at ICL 13, 42, 62, 77–94
 organisational 1–2, 11, 81, 82, 92,
  98, 115–16, 117, 135, 136
 in role of personnel function
  135–7

technological 3–4, 6–7, 17, 55–6,
 80–81, 82, 136
 in workforce 136
 in work patterns 80–81, 84, 103
clients, internal
 identification of 19–25
 interviews with 29, 39–41, 84–5
 measuring satisfaction 19, 29,
  39–41, 63
 meeting needs 19–22, 42, 48, 49,
  50, 126, 130, 137
climate audit 27
codes of practice 17, 34, 44
communications
 electronic systems 80–81
 policies 29, 52
 strategies 17, 93, 138–9
company employment history
 reports
 Edmund Nuttall Ltd 130
competencies/competency
 modelling 114–23
computerised systems
 audit 38–9
 Edmund Nuttall Ltd 127
 ICL 80–81, 82
 standards 93
 KLM Royal Dutch Arlines
  95–106
 new developments 17, 20, 80–81,
  82
 potential underutilised 3–4, 6–7,
  20, 138
 quality principles 63
 skill profiling and employee
  assessment (Bull UK) 114,
  118–21
Connock, S. 30
constraints, identification of 17
consultants 27–8
continuous improvement 11, 12, 46,
 79
cost/benefit analysis 8–9, 137
cost centre reports
 Edmund Nuttall Ltd 131